Go Back to
School
& Get Better

It was a pleasure meeting.
I hope this book inspired you to be
even greater in your educational journey

CHANDRA KYDD

From the U.S.

authorHOUSE®

AuthorHouse™
1663 Liberty Drive
Bloomington, IN 47403
www.authorhouse.com
Phone: 833-262-8899

Published by AuthorHouse 08/08/2024

ISBN: 979-8-8230-2978-0 (sc)
ISBN: 979-8-8230-2979-7 (hc)
ISBN: 979-8-8230-2977-3 (e)

Library of Congress Control Number: 2024913704

Print information available on the last page.

Quotes to Inspire

"The best thing you can do for a child is teach their parents so they can provide more time and resources to their kids."
By: Chandra Kydd

Start by doing what's necessary; then do what's possible, and suddenly, you are doing the impossible."
By: Francis of Assisi

"The secret of getting ahead is getting started."
By: Mark Twain

"You will never profit from excuses because no one buys them."
By: Chandra Kydd

"I did then what I knew how to do. Now that I know better, I do better."
By: Maya Angelou

"The individual who says it is not possible should move out of the way of those doing it."
By: Tricia Cunningham

"Education is what remains after one has forgotten what one has learned in school."
By: Albert Einstein

"If 'Plan A' didn't work, the alphabet has 25 more letters! Stay Cool."
By: Unknown

Contents

Demystifying the GED®: A Comprehensive Overview and Evolution

Isn't a GED® a dummy's diploma? Absolutely *NOT!* The General Education Development (GED®) was created to determine if adults have the academic skills equivalent to that of a high school senior. There is a stigma that the GED® is a "lesser than" exam. Many believe it is a subpar alternative to a traditional high school diploma. The GED® has only one significant difference- it does not list the name of a public or private high school; instead, it is issued directly from that state's Department of Education. In other words, it's the same diploma minus a high school name.

The test measures proficiency in critical areas, including Math, Science, Social Studies, and Reasoning through Language Arts (RLA). Beyond assessing foundational knowledge, it also evaluates additional college and career readiness elements such as critical thinking, logic, keyboarding, and digital literacy, making it a robust measure of academic readiness for the 21st century. If a student successfully passes all parts of the exam, they will receive their high school diploma in the mail, and if those grads need transcripts, they can order them to be shipped as well.

According to GED® Testing Service, "It all started during World War II when the credential was created to make it easier for veterans to pick up where they left off with their plans for education, careers, and personal goals. In 1942, the United States Armed Forces Institute (USAFI) launched the GED®." The GED® program expanded to civilians in the 1950s, creating a much-needed avenue for adults without a traditional high school education. This alternative allowed for further education and a pathway for personal and career development.

Historically, school attendance among adolescents was not always a priority in this country; family sizes tended to be significant, and children were often expected to work to bring income into the household. Kids usually worked in factories, mines, and within agriculture industries for less pay than adults at hours just as tedious as their grown-up co-workers. It was typical for a child as young as seven to work a 12-hour, 6-day work week.

With earning money being such a focus and education being so far down the list of priorities, it's easy to see why some may have struggled to finish school in years past. The problem with this system was that as industries grew, so did the demand for managers and entrepreneurs with the skills to innovate and lead employees. Lawmakers saw the need to shift from a labor-driven focus to an education-driven one. Companies sought workers who could read, write, do math, and use critical thinking to solve problems. They demanded staff who could do more than work with their hands. They needed a workforce to strategize, analyze data, comprehend written materials, and function without constant supervision. Of course, employees who could meet these demands could negotiate higher wages, benefits, and promotions.

Later, these tests were also administered in Federal correctional facilities and health institutions. "The GED® became so popular among civilians that the organization adjusted its name to encompass a wide variety of students." (GED® Testing Service) The documented roots underscore its importance in providing opportunities for these diverse groups.

The curriculum targets of the test have also evolved in several ways throughout history. It grew as the needs of the industry changed. In the 1970s, the focus shifted from requiring students to recall general facts to preparing them for education *beyond* high school. Then, in the 80s, it was reformed by adding a written component that did not exist before, incorporating socially relevant topics with more problem-solving questions to prepare examinees for higher-level employment positions. If we fast forward to the early 2000s, it became increasingly rigorous by infusing more business-related content, requiring students to explain and interpret science experiments. It integrated more multicultural content to reflect the large number of immigrants taking the exam, and the passages contained were lengthened and higher level. The GED® has continued to be inclusive, with testing services available at various locations, ensuring accessibility for multiple populations.

The content was not the only revision made. The number of subjects and the modality in which the test was administered were updated. The test was previously paper-based, but it's now computer-based. The new format has brought to light the need for students to have digital literacy skills. So, some students may do well with the content but struggle to maneuver the technology, especially since questions are not all multiple-choice. Additional formats include drag and drop, hot spot, and fill-in-the-blank questions. Plus, there is the extended response essay, which requires knowledge of keyboarding, scrolling, and clicking and dragging. These technological configurations enhance the assessment's relevance to real-world scenarios. An added benefit of the computer-based exam is that results are typically provided within minutes instead of four to six weeks or results being lost, as was the case with the paper-based exam.

Depending on which state you live in, you may need to take one of the following assessments to get your diploma: HiSET = Hish School Equivalency Test, TASC = Test Assessing Secondary Completion, or GED Testing Service = General Education Development. The presence of various testing companies provides states with alternatives tailored to their educational priorities. However, ensuring consistency across states and avoiding confusion among test takers may require a streamlined approach to testing options. For example, Florida is a GED Testing Service state, so students within Florida must pass all four subjects of that exam to obtain their high school diploma. If they move to another state that offers HiSET or TASC, they will have to pass all the subjects of those exams to get their credential. So, test takers cannot mix and match tests, even if they have only one subject remaining.

The GED® program has proven to be a dynamic and crucial resource for individuals seeking educational attainment beyond the traditional high school pathway. By dispelling the myth of its inferiority and emphasizing its historical roots, adaptability, and inclusivity, this book aims to highlight the positive impact of the GED® on the lives of countless individuals. Continuous improvements could be made to address computer literacy challenges and harmonize testing options to enhance the program's effectiveness in facilitating educational and career advancement for diverse populations.

Section 1

The Adult Students

Chapter 1

No More Shoulda, Coulda, Woulda's
(Get up and go back to school)

What are you waiting for? What's the reason you've delayed going back to school? Is it your work schedule, debt, family obligations, illness, or lack of motivation? Whatever the rationale, it may hold you back from making more income or seizing more significant opportunities that would benefit you and your family. My primary goal is to motivate people to seek higher education. While it primarily focuses on obtaining a high school diploma, its aim extends beyond that to inspire individuals to pursue various post-secondary degrees, certifications, or even non-traditional learning opportunities. I could sugar-coat why you should run to your nearest adult education learning center and start your journey to get your diploma or degree, but I won't. You picked this book up for a reason. You know deep within yourself that you have been putting off this worthwhile decision for some time. Or maybe you know someone who needs a little push or a big shove in the right direction. This book aims to be that shove. Use it, share it, or both, but its purpose is to help someone "Get Better."

I have had many students, friends, and family members ask me to personally reach out to someone they know and convince that individual to go back to school. While I have done it more times than I can remember, I realized that I can't call, email, or meet everyone who may need that one-on-one conversation to help them decide to go for it! I hope this book inspires the masses that I would never reach one at a time. This resource contains stories of real people who made the leap and went back and how that decision changed their lives. Some of these students followed the path to the finish line.

On the other hand, others fell prey to some form of distraction or life-altering situation. Fictitious names have been used to protect identities. Still, their stories are meant to show you that you can do it and are not alone in the struggles of wanting to accomplish this goal.

Wasting Time Means Losing Money

It's no secret we all see the drastic rise in the cost of living and necessities such as food, utilities, transportation, and housing. But have you considered the accelerating cost of education? While you prolong going back to school, everyday expenses and post-secondary schooling continue to increase. According to the U.S. Bureau of Labor Statistics, "Prices for college tuition and fees increased 4.7 percent from February 2020 to February 2023. Over the same time, this increase was less than the 15.7 percent in prices for other items, such as groceries. From February 2020 to February 2023, prices for technical and business school tuition and fees rose 5.2 percent." Surprisingly, costs for obtaining a high school diploma have shown a slow and low increase, with most adult education institutions ranging from free to $50 per term (terms last four months). That's a small investment for a credential that can potentially get you a significant pay increase. "In 2022, for example, workers aged 25 and over without a high school diploma had median weekly earnings of $682. However, workers whose highest level of education was a diploma made $853 per week, or just over 25 percent more than those who didn't finish high school—and earnings improved with every level of education completed." (U.S. Bureau of Labor Statistics) (See chart.)

Earnings and unemployment rates by educational attainment, 2022

Median usual weekly earnings   Unemployment rate

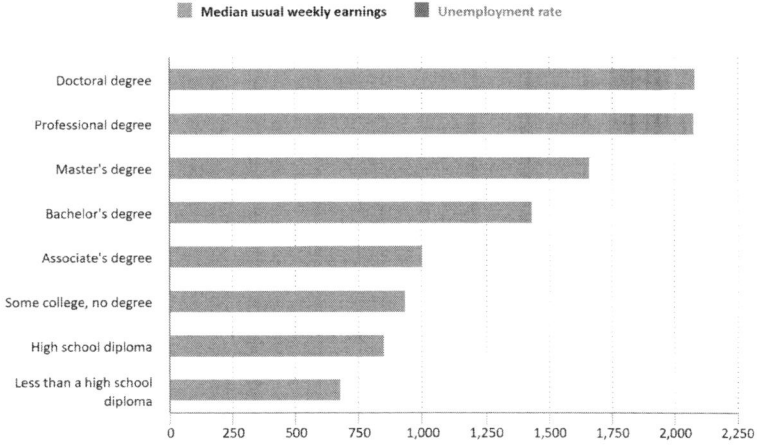

Click legend items to change data display. Hover over chart to view data.
Note: Data are for persons age 25 and over. Earnings are for full-time wage and salary workers.
Source: U.S. Bureau of Labor Statistics, Current Population Survey.

Let's use this chart's data to determine how much a person could have earned if they had gotten their high school diploma sooner. Imagine our example, Lisa. Lisa had planned to return to school three years ago but delayed it due to "life getting in the way." Without a diploma, Lisa makes approximately $682 weekly. If Lisa had her diploma, she could have been making about $853, giving her a loss of $171 per week. Let's multiply that by 36 months (the three years she didn't have her diploma). Overall, Lisa lost $6,156 in prospective pay doing the same job because she waited to return to school. Consider how much Lisa could have purchased or paid for with those funds. Not to mention, the cost of tuition could have risen if she intended to go for a higher level of education, plus the potential loss for those pay increases. In the end, Lisa lost not only time but also money.

Some people delay going back to school because they are not sure what field to study. I know of many people who pick a career because their parents or relatives want them to go into that industry, so the student is only selecting that certification to please others. Keep in mind, whichever field you choose, you are the one to arise each morning and do that job until retirement. So, choose what you want to do. Not sure what that is? Here are a couple of websites that will engage you in career exploration, by asking you some questions about your likes/dislikes, talents and interests: *mynextmove.org* & *onetonline.org*

It's About More than the Money

Beyond the increased earning potential are the benefits of personal growth and self-improvement. I have had many students who were not seeking job advancement. They were already employed in their field of choice or business owners. Yet, they enrolled to reach a bar they had always intended to master. That will boost your confidence and self-esteem, making you better equipped to tackle other challenges in life.

For instance, I had a student we'll refer to as Marcus, a very accomplished track and field athlete when he was younger. He had great success in his sport and used that tenacity to build his business. He did well for himself financially, and his businesses, yes, I said *businesses*, were growing. However, his competitive and perfectionist nature caused turmoil because he never got his diploma. So, in his mind, he did not have all the success he sought. Marcus and I had a great discussion about the importance of being mentally prepared for life's challenges. He shared with me a story about a race he competed in. He provided me with the background about what a false start was (when a runner starts the race before the sound of the starting gun) and how the rules, at the time, stipulated that there could only be up to 3 restarts of a race due to a false start before you were disqualified.

Marcus was confident in his ability to win, but another runner had a false start. When the race started again, a second runner had a false start. That second false start caused his inner thoughts to give up on winning because he became frustrated that he had put so much energy into two races that he could not win because of the mistakes of those two other runners. So, before the start of the third attempt, he had told himself, "Just forget it." Unfortunately, since he had mentally given way to those negative thoughts, he lost. Marcus has carried that defeat with him and regrets it deeply, even after so many years have passed.

While teaching the skills a student will encounter on an exam is essential, motivating them is an even greater task as an adult educator.

If students lose enthusiasm, the likelihood of them giving up increases significantly. For this reason, I often dive deep into one-on-one conversations about why they chose to return to school and why they left in the first place. This investigation gives me valuable insight into what drives them. In Marcus's case, he was not satisfied with the prospect of never reaching this symbolic finish line, which he found unacceptable. He expressed that losing the race should not have happened because he was beyond skilled in his technique and physically prepared to win that competition. Despite his preparation, his mental fortitude had shifted to the negative during the tournament, making success impossible. However, that inner competitive spirit made him vow that this race to obtain his diploma was one he planned to finish strong!

Most students who start but do not finish often wish they had gotten it done earlier to take advantage of opportunities that come into view. For example, Doris, who was in her 60s, shared that she had been trying to get her diploma off and on for several years. She attributed the extended timeframe to her raising six children alone. Doris would register, get busy and overwhelmed, and then stop. Once things seemed to be a bit better, she'd return to school. The cycle repeated until she realized she had been doing this for several years and had not progressed much.

There were job opportunities that she wanted to apply for. While she had all the mandated certifications and licenses for the job, she did not have her diploma. It was always the first item listed on the requirements of the position. Doris knew these lost opportunities equated to thousands of dollars in wages she could have made to help support herself and her kids. She declared she was tired of the in-and-out routine and wouldn't leave until she got what she came for. You can imagine the joy Doris felt when she passed her first exam. She is still going strong, and I am proud to be a part of her journey toward becoming a graduate for herself and an example to her grandchildren.

Choose Your Hard

Life presents various challenges that can often feel overwhelming. Some people struggle with low-income, lack of employment opportunities, time management issues, and lack of family support. These things are "hard" and highly stressful, but you do it anyway. Whenever I converse with someone claiming they need to return to school, I ask them, "What's the hold-up?" Their first response, usually in a saddened tone, is, "Things are so hard right now." So, I look them directly in the eyes and ask, "How long are you willing to live with '*this hard?*'" They get shocked by that. They immediately stop pouting because no one has ever said it to their face in such a bold manner. While they may have never thought of it that way, they instantly ponder how much more of their current situation they can take. As they think it through, their tone changes from despair to hope because now they start to visualize the possibilities that can come from moving forward in education over remaining stagnant in their complicated situation.

These hardships can lead individuals to feel stuck in a cycle of difficulties. However, pursuing higher education can serve as a transformative path toward a brighter future. Individuals can effectively address and potentially alleviate their challenges by opting for the path of returning to school and obtaining a diploma or higher degree. This decision signifies a commitment to personal growth. It opens doors to increased employment opportunities, financial stability, and an improved quality of life for them and their family.

The fear of failure can overshadow skills preparation. In a scenario, let's consider a student named Janice who had diligently prepared for her GED® Language test for weeks. Despite putting in long hours of study and review, she found herself consumed by overwhelming anxiety and fear as the exam day approached.

Her fear of failure and self-doubt grew so intense that it affected her concentration. On the exam day, Janice's mind went blank as she stared at the questions in front of her. The fear of not performing well paralyzed her, leading to a mental block that prevented her from recalling the information she had worked so hard to learn.

As a result, Janice struggled to answer the questions effectively, making mistakes that she knew were uncharacteristic of her true capabilities. The fear and anxiety she experienced not only hindered her performance during the exam but also left her feeling defeated and disappointed in herself afterward.

One skill that I taught my students was how to create an effective vision board *(I have a 2-part video on my YouTube channel that explains how to create one)*. I did this because I know it does not matter how much study you put in if you are not mentally ready for success. Vision boards can be powerful instruments to help people "see" those things they want to manifest in their future. While all students put items like conquering their tests and getting their diploma on their boards, others added things such as job advancement, weddings, dream homes, cars, and better lifestyle habits like diet and exercise.

It was amazing how quickly students started coming to class and sharing stories of how the things on their boards were coming to pass almost immediately. For instance, one student got a promotion at work the same day she took her board home, another got an engagement ring from her boyfriend three days after putting it on her board, and one student's credit score jumped a massive amount of points within days of including it on hers. Multiple students passed their GED® tests just like they demonstrated on their boards. They were so excited at the results that they asked me to create a way to explain the concept to their family and friends about how to do it, so I made a couple of videos on my Facebook and YouTube pages for them to share with others.

Your mindset can either open or close the door to your future. If you are of the attitude that it's just too hard, then you're right. It's just too hard for you, but the moment you put that thinking to rest and get to work, what seemed too hard becomes doable and then done! If you tell yourself that you can have the very thing you see yourself having, that is correct. You will have precisely what your mind limits you to have. That's why it is important to watch out for the dream killers (I'll explain them in a later chapter).

Consider Sarah, a determined individual who found herself struggling to juggle multiple jobs, limited career prospects, and financial instability. Recognizing that her current situation was a significant roadblock to her aspirations, she boldly decided to return to school to further her education. Despite facing initial doubts and obstacles, Sarah's dedication and perseverance paid off as she completed her diploma program. With newfound knowledge and skills, Sarah landed a rewarding job that provided financial security and career growth. Her decision to embrace the challenge of pursuing higher education transformed her life. It positively impacted her family by setting an inspiring example of resilience and determination for future generations.

The Comfort of Excuses

Excuses are like a balm to soothe the torment of someone not doing what they know they should be doing. They are the stories we tell ourselves to justify not getting things done, and they make total sense to the person giving them. Those excuses are often followed by promises to do them later. Here is a list of the typical reasons a person gives to explain why they have delayed going back to school:

- "I'm too tired."
- "It's the middle of the week, so I'll start Monday."
- "I'll start in the new year."
- "It's not my fault."
- "I've been out of school too long."
- "I'm not smart enough"
- "I'm too old."
- "I don't have the money right now."
- "I can't because I have kids."
- "I don't have enough time."
- "I don't have a car."
- "I don't have a job."
- "I'm too busy."
- "I'm not a citizen"
- "I have a criminal record"
- "I'm too nervous."
- "I'm too scared."

Putting off for later what could be accomplished now is called *procrastination,* commonly labeled "dragging your feet." Don't confuse procrastination with laziness. They are two different things. "Procrastination is an active process – you choose to do something else instead of the task you know you should be doing. In contrast, laziness suggests apathy, inactivity, and an unwillingness to act." (MindTools) A person may give excuses for both. Still, procrastination can lead to mental issues such as guilt and anxiety, primarily after you reflect on the choice you made NOT to be productive. It can also damage your reputation in the eyes of others.

Stop Procrastinating

By postponing your essential task, you have also delayed the rewards of those actions. Procrastinating on specific events may even lead to consequences. How do you overcome such a bad habit? First, stop putting things off. Just get started and don't stop until the job is complete.

Also, you can organize what you need to take care of by the level of importance or the time it will take to complete it. Let's say I was planning to clean my home. I might list all the chores I need to do, starting with the tasks that are quickest to complete and saving the more time-consuming duties for later. Once I see several items checked off, it may motivate me to finish more items on my to-do list. On the other hand, I could sort my list by order of importance. For instance, the more pressing duty may be getting my laundry done. Then, I would tackle the other responsibilities accordingly. This technique of sorting events in a structured manner gives you a plan to tackle them and encourages you to see the list through to completion.

Another strategy is to minimize distractions once you start. For example, if you plan to study, turn off possible interruptions like the phone and television and ask others not to disturb you for the time you need to focus. I talked with a student regarding his lack of study time while his children were home. I recommended he establish an indicator to let his children know when it was not okay to bother Dad. I suggested he get a bright and colorful tie from his collection and call it the "quiet-time flag."

He was to place that tie around the doorknob when he needed to study each evening. So, when the kids saw it, they knew not to enter the room or make too much noise. However, I expressed how important it would be to get them in bed at a consistent time to help him plan his study schedule around moments after they were asleep.

It would not be fair to have the "quiet-time flag" posted all day, every day. I told him to make sure he intentionally planned some fun time with them so the kids did not feel like they lost their dad because he had decided to return to school. Incorporating this strategy rewarded the children for allowing Daddy the space to work. In return, he got some needed study time each evening.

Don't Blame the Kids; Do It for the Kids

It is important to avoid using our children as an excuse to put off striving to get a better education. It will not be easy. Trust me, I know. I got my master's degree with three children under ten years old. Juggling school and children will require a solid, yet consistently balanced routine, especially bedtime. I had to balance 9-hour workdays, three kids, two dogs, a husband (at the time), master's degree courses, and a household (cooking, cleaning, laundry, etc.). It was challenging, and it took me a while to catch the rhythm I needed not to feel overwhelmed, but failure was not an option.

Since my kids were young, they wanted my attention *a lot*. Kids do not truly understand the reasons and benefits of their parents returning to school. You must be patient with them and reassure them that they are still a priority to you, and this routine shift will only be temporary. After all, one of the biggest motivations to finish your education could be to provide a better life for your children. They are worth it! Plus, you become their role model about the importance of education. If they hear you saying they must do their level best in school, yet they see you not giving your best effort, that contradiction can be hypocritical to your message. Kids do as you do, not just what you say.

No Time Like the Present

The problem with planning to finish school later is that life is unpredictable. I once had a 20-year-old student named Angeline enrolled in my social studies and reading classes. She told me how her dad pushed her to change from her old ways of slacking on her academics to finishing school before she reached 21. He told her if she made the deadline, which was almost one year away, he would help her buy a car. With that incentive, she found a new excitement about the prospect of turning her life around for the better. She started off doing well, but after a month, her motto became, "I got a year. That's more than enough time to get it done". With that in mind, Angeline started slacking off again. She kept saying, "I got time. I'll get it done." I constantly had to remind her that watching videos in class was prohibited. I also reiterated that studying was essential to making fast progress whenever I noticed her making a poor effort or missing class "on purpose." But, again, I heard, "I got time. I'll get it done."

One day, Angeline's dad called me, which was not unusual because he and I had spoken multiple times about strategies to help keep her motivated, but this conversation was different. He was very somber and had difficulty speaking. When I asked what was wrong, he told me that his daughter had died in a car accident.

She had been in the backseat of a friend's car when it had careened into a canal near their home. She was not able to get out of her seatbelt and drowned. Her father was devastated by the loss and how sudden it had all been. He, too, had heard her say, "I got time, I'll get it done." But now, there was no more time to get it done. I was saddened that I would not have the chance to see her walk the stage.

Then, there was Isabella, a single mom from Ecuador. She had little support in the U.S. but was eager to improve her English and get a diploma in her new country. She was so kind to her classmates and always sat in the front. Isabella's limited English made her very quiet, but she never hesitated to participate in assignments, class projects, and discussions. Plus, she always finished her homework on time. She was a model student. Based on her class performance, I encouraged her to take the test, but she kept putting it off and saying, "Teacher, I'm not ready." I had her take the official practice test, and she scored well beyond passing, but still, she was convinced she was not ready to test.

Isabella never missed school until she began to have these excruciating headaches. She constantly apologized for missing class, but she had a difficult time with the headaches coming and going. I told her not to be afraid and to take the test, but she said she needed more time to prepare. After a few weeks of struggling to function with headaches, she began to get blurred vision. I asked Isabella why she refused to go to the doctor for a checkup. She said she didn't have insurance or anyone to watch her 8-year-old son if she had to go to an appointment. I let her know that the hospital would treat her even if she didn't have insurance, so she finally agreed and promised to keep me posted.

A few weeks later, Isabella called the school to speak to me. She said she had gone to the emergency room, and they discovered a brain tumor. Hence, the doctors wanted to perform surgery to try to remove it. She was so scared because she had no health insurance, couldn't afford to take time off from work, and especially because she had no family to help care for her son and get him to school after her surgery. I made her promise to keep me posted about her procedure and any help she may need. Unfortunately, I never heard back to know how things fared, and her number was no longer in service when I tried to call.

These are more extreme examples of how putting off for tomorrow what can be done today can be derailed. On the other hand, there are countless accounts of students who, with the best intentions, stopped making progress because of changes in their work schedule, such as job loss or new employment opportunities. When these occasions occur, it can be years before they go back to pick up where they left off. At that point, the person feels as if they are starting all over again because they have forgotten all they had learned before they stopped attending classes. Their typical first words are, "I wish I would have gotten it over with back then." The regret they walk through the door with shows on their face, but I welcome them with open arms and tell them to focus on the present and move forward.

When they return, they often come back with a deeper understanding of the economic difficulty of life without a high school diploma or the lack of a post-secondary education credential. As a result of that realization, they are more diligent in their pursuit of success. I learned years ago that to teach an individual, they must see the value in what the teacher is offering. There's the saying, "You can lead a horse to water, but you can't make it drink." The same is valid for education. A teacher can provide all the information and resources, but they can't make a person want its benefits.

Expanding your Knowledge and Enhancing your Critical Thinking and Problem-Solving Skills Gives you an Advantage.

I mentioned that the essence of the exam is to determine if individuals possess the skills needed for success in college and their careers. So, one of the reasons the test has evolved to its rigorous standards is that many higher education institutions and industry leaders have appealed to decision-makers within the education department to ensure students obtain the critical thinking skills needed to function in high-stakes situations.

Let's look at their perspective on why these qualities are critical. In the beginning of the book, I discussed how the economy shifted from one that wanted skilled laborers to one that needed managers and entrepreneurs. The most significant part of these advanced positions is the ability to use critical thinking to solve problems that could emerge daily. Company CEOs do not want to have to micromanage their managers or tell them how to oversee operations all day long. The supervisor's purpose is to ensure operations go smoothly within their department. If trouble does arise, they will have the capacity to act quickly to mitigate the issue so that it does not put the overall company at risk.

Not every person can think on their feet and make split-second decisions, especially if the situation puts lives at risk. Companies seek this level of problem-solving skills and are willing to pay accordingly to obtain them. Respectively, the more people you oversee, the more money you make. Let's imagine a few scenarios to drive the point home.

Imagine a hospital losing power and being damaged during a severe storm. Who will make the decisions to ensure employees are safe, patients still get the care they need, lifesaving equipment is preserved, and lives are not lost because of the power outage? When dealing with emergency healthcare, every minute counts. Let's try this scenario: a construction company loses one of its biggest suppliers, yet the contracted deadline to finish the project is quickly approaching. Who will know how to rectify the situation efficiently to get construction back on track and meet the client's deadline? These, and many others, are the jobs of managers who must have a knack for critical thinking and confidence in their decision-making abilities.

How about we look at it from a higher education point of view? Post-secondary institutions are competitive, just like any other business. Let's use XYZ University, with a student population of 25,000, as an example. Their goal is to ensure those who enroll finish and receive their credentials. It is harmful to them to have high dropout rates at their school. "While high school dropout rates are decreasing, the United States experiences a daunting 40% college dropout rate yearly. With only 41% of students graduating after four years without delay, American universities tend to pale at the scale of this recurring issue" (ThinkImpact, 2021). This is a very high percentage of students paying for an education they may not complete. So, this could mean a student does not get a sufficient return on their educational investment since they may walk away with student loan debt but not a higher-level degree.

So why is there such a high percentage of students not meeting the goal of graduating college? Of course, there are many, but "Academic pressure accounts for 28% of college dropouts, as students may be unprepared or unequipped for the challenges of university-level schooling" (ThinkImpact, 2021). With statistics such as these, getting students across the finish line becomes more difficult for XYZ University, which can affect other vital components to the school's success, such as remaining competitive with other schools and having a sufficient completion rate to maintain its accreditation. With these things in mind, it would be helpful if students came through the door better equipped with the skills needed to function at the college level.

With a population of over 25,000 students, if 40% of them struggle to maintain an acceptable GPA towards graduation, that could equate to over 10,000 students (about the seating capacity of Cameron basketball stadium at Duke University) at risk. Why should you care about all of this? No one wants to be a part of the statistical 40% who do not get their degree. The best way to avoid being on the negative side of the statistics is to work diligently to ensure you have the academic and motivational skills needed to handle the more intense demands of post-secondary education. In addition, soft skills like consistent attendance, being organized, and studying for your classes will be make-or-break issues.

Imagine John, a dedicated student who decided to pursue a degree in business administration while working full-time and managing a busy family life. During his studies, he learned valuable problem-solving techniques and gained in-depth knowledge about effective communication and leadership skills.

One day at work, John encountered a complex issue where his team struggled to meet tight deadlines and conflicting priorities. Drawing upon his education, he quickly identified the key obstacles, organized a strategic plan, and effectively communicated with his team members to delegate tasks and streamline the workflow. Not only did they meet the deadline successfully, but John's proactive problem-solving approach also earned him recognition from his superiors.

In his personal life, John faced a challenging situation where a family conflict was causing tension and misunderstandings. Applying the conflict resolution strategies he learned in his education, John approached the issue calmly, listened actively to all parties involved, and facilitated a constructive dialogue to reach a positive resolution. His newfound skills helped mend relationships within his family. They improved his well-being and sense of fulfillment outside work and school.

Confidence Comes from Accomplishment, and Confidence Empowers

Who doesn't like feeling good? Confidence is the full belief and trust in oneself. It is obvious when a person either has it or lacks it. It is evident in how we speak, walk, and carry ourselves. It is noticeable by family, friends, and even strangers. The lack of confidence and fear usually go hand in hand. The sense of accomplishment and achieving goals boosts poise because it reinforces the idea that you can do whatever you put your mind to. I often tell my students that the resume gets them the interview, but it is frequently the interview that gets you the job. The poise you show and the way you present yourself during an interview can outweigh the skills (or lack thereof) on your resume.

There are attributes employers are looking for beyond credentials. Indeed.com lists 15 top qualities employers want in an employee. Confidence is rated #3, and critical thinking is #4. The two noted at the top are ambition and communication. Guess what? Problem-solving is on the list too!

Marcus, who lost the race, did not just lose a physical race but also a level of self-assurance. His mindset had shifted from what it was, so it psychologically threw things *off track* for him. How do we combat this? Get more wins! You must have the grit to persevere when things get tough. Don't forget there is a prize at the end of it.

Feeling good about yourself is priceless and affects every aspect of your life, so why not strive to have it in abundance? Preparation increases confidence, and confidence can overshadow fear and anxiety, making it possible to accomplish even more. It becomes like a domino effect. The more you win, the more you *want* to win and take it to the next level.

Greater education can significantly boost your confidence and happiness. When you learn, you sharpen your skills, expand your knowledge, and achieve milestones that make you proud of yourself. Education empowers you by providing the tools and abilities to overcome challenges and excel in various aspects of life. Here are a few reasons why pursuing higher education can lead to increased confidence:

- Increased Knowledge: Education enhances your understanding of the world, giving you a sense of mastery and confidence in your abilities.
- Skill Development: Learning new skills and improving existing ones can boost your self-confidence, because it makes you feel more capable of taking on new challenges.
- Achieving Goals: Setting and accomplishing educational goals can give you a sense of fulfillment and pride, boosting your self-esteem.
- Networking Opportunities: Education opens doors to new connections and relationships, which can enhance your confidence and overall happiness.
- Career Advancement: Higher education can lead to better job opportunities and a sense of career success, contributing to your overall confidence and well-being.

Imagine Sarah, a working adult who decided to return to school to pursue a degree in psychology. Initially, she was nervous about balancing work, family, and school responsibilities. However, as she progressed in her studies and felt more self-assured in her abilities and knowledge. Completing challenging assignments and receiving positive feedback from her professors boosted her self-esteem. Sarah's increased self-belief helped her excel academically and translated into other areas of her life, making her happier and more fulfilled.

Chapter 2

The Ultimate Pillow Fight

"Sorry, I'm late. I have trouble getting out of bed in the mornings." These are the words I often hear when someone was absent the previous day or late for the 8 am class. If your bed is anything like mine, it has built-in magnets that tend to hold you deep within its soft, cozy blankets and cloud-fluffy pillows. I am not speaking to those with some meaningful reason to be late, such as dropping off kids to school, immediate family members to work, or coming to school directly from your night shift. I am talking about those who struggle with waking up in the mornings. You must discipline yourself to get up and get to school on time. If your morning work shift begins at 8 am, you would most likely arrive at your scheduled time or risk the security of your position, so it is imperative to use the same diligence towards getting up and out the door for school.

The aim should be to reach your objective within a reasonable amount of time so you can move on to the next step toward your ultimate goal-greater wisdom and better employment opportunities. The number one question students ask me is, "How long will it take for me to get my diploma?" While everyone will take different amounts of time to complete the GED® process, it does not have to take several years to get it done. I have seen some students earn their diplomas in as little as a month while others took several years. It all depends on your level of commitment and consistency.

The More You Attend, the Faster you Move

It is common knowledge that the more you attend class, the greater your chances are of reaching the finish line in a timely manner. "Although it is not the only factor, research shows that class attendance is positively related to subsequent academic performance. Attendance has been linked to higher exam performance" (Jeff Bergin and Lisa Ferrara). If you struggle to pass your exams, reflect on how often you attend class. In addition to that, look at your consistency when you study.

I've had more students than I can count who must retest a subject several times because they are not putting in consistent class and study time. Remember, the test determines if an individual has the functional skills necessary to excel in a college and career arena. So, students need to be in an environment where they can learn and practice those skills to achieve mastery. This comment is not geared towards the person with a legitimate obligation, such as a work schedule that conflicts with their school schedule or a sick child they must stay home to care for. However, I am referring to those who could go to class but choose to "skip it" from a mindset of "I don't feel like it."

Under-Agers

Young people are legally mandated to be enrolled in high school until age 16 to avoid truancy, after which they can withdraw. The reality is thousands of teens do not have a high school diploma. Those students may choose (or be forced) to transition to adult ed. Unlike high school, there are no report cards and parents cannot be informed of the student's progress without written consent from the student. However, that adult institution must support this special demographic and help them meet their goal.

I had a 17-year-old student named Clarence who registered for class because his parents gave him an ultimatum that he must either be enrolled in school or move out of the house. He was usually late and often complained about how much he hated to get up in the mornings to go to school. He showed up often enough to remain active on the roster but eventually stopped coming. Clarence returned a few years later and appeared so exhausted and in despair. When I saw his face, I immediately asked what was wrong. He shared that his parents had divorced, which made his mother a single mom who had to take care of him and his siblings alone. As a result, he now needed to help his mom financially to avoid them losing their house. He said he regretted not getting it over with years before. He admitted that he wasn't motivated to finish then because he was comfortable with his parents providing everything. His lack of persistent participation made it easy to go from coming to class occasionally to not at all.

Unfortunately, some younger students struggle with issues like unplugging from personal devices or having the self-discipline to follow through on the steps needed to get things done efficiently. An important aspect of adult ed. is the need for students to take ownership of their progress. If they are under 18, they cannot legally take the GED® test until specific requirements are met. Every state may have different processes, so please refer to your school district's guidelines for more information.

Young People are the Future

Please note that not all underage students come to adult ed. lacking the motivation to do well and gain their credentials quickly. Since they were more recently enrolled in a traditional school setting, they tend to pass their tests in fewer attempts. I have had hundreds of young people excited about having an alternative to the conventional track toward graduation.

One such student sticks out in my mind- Clark. This young man came to class on day one, ready to go. He was very formal in how he spoke and approached me to introduce himself and shake my hand. Clark sat right in front and took out his pen and a notebook, ready to receive whatever I might throw at him. Yet, I could tell he was trying to feel me out to see if I would be like some instructors of his past. He shared that he'd had previous teachers who did not treat him in a manner he felt was supportive or challenged him enough for his skill level, which is why the traditional path didn't work for him. This kid was smart! I enjoyed him the moment he responded to my first question.

When I had the chance, I asked him what he planned to do after getting his diploma. He jumped at the opportunity to pull out this special notebook he carried around with him, which contained this elaborate blueprint about this invention he planned to build and put on the market to sell. It was apparent he had done tons of research and was on fire about his vision for his future. He even had projections on his future profits. He was so intense that I wanted to be the first investor! Clark was so fierce that I wanted to drop the twenty I had in my pocket on the table just to back it up and show him how confident I was that he would make it the way he planned! At that moment, I took it upon myself to do whatever I could to throw logs on the fire burning within him because potential and passion of this magnitude should never be allowed to burn out. I could feel I was in the presence of a future mogul.

I had another brilliant 17-year-old student I met when I ran out to grab lunch. He noticed my school's logo on my shirt and asked if I knew anything about the GED® program. I introduced myself and gave him a superfast overview of what he needed to do to enroll. I gave him my card and told him to find me on campus, and I'd explain in more detail if he so desired. I ran out the door back to work and was pleasantly surprised when he showed up the next day to talk with me. He was Vietnamese and had been homeschooled all his life, but he wanted to transition to formal schooling to get his diploma. He admitted that he was not sure how his parents would react to his wishes but felt comfortable enough with me to see if I'd be willing to explain the process to them.

I didn't hesitate to set up a meeting time. Ultimately, that young man enrolled and passed every subject with some of the highest scores I'd seen. Despite all that genius he had going for himself, the family had many struggles that made his journey difficult, but he made it! In some Asian cultures, it is not customary for them to look directly into a person's eyes or enter another's personal space, so when he ran to hug me and then gave a bow to me on the graduation stage to say thank you, the show of gratitude set the crowd wild. Graduation has always been emotional for me, but what he did made me bawl like a baby on stage in front of everyone. His parents also came and saluted me and shook my hand after the ceremony.

"Attendance is about more than showing up to class or an event— it can provide indications of student motivation, participation, time management, and adherence to program or institutional expectations."

(Jeff Bergin and Lisa Ferrara) When you get into the habit of NOT going to school, you accumulate gaps in your learning and understanding, and it can almost begin to feel like you must start repeatedly. Over time, constant restarting can lead to frustration and thoughts of the process being too hard or impossible.

How to Win the Pillow Fight

Adjusting to something new takes consistency over time. Eventually, it gets easier because the body will adapt to the new routine. Here are some tips to help you get up in the mornings:

- Set an alarm, even on weekends and holidays.
- Gradually increase your wake-up time by setting your alarm when you usually wake up, then adjust your wake-up time by 15 minutes every day until you reach your desired time. For instance, say you typically get up at 10 am, but you *need* to get up at 8 am, set your alarm 15 minutes earlier every day: 10 am, then 9:45 am, then 9:30, and so on, until you work your way up to 8 am.
- Get a bedtime routine that allows you to wind down before sleep. Examples include reading, meditating, enjoying a hot tea, turning the lights down low, or a warm bath to signal your body that it's time for bed.
- Get enough rest during the night so you are refreshed in the morning. Aim for 7-9 hours to recharge your mind and body to be energized the following day.
- Do NOT hit the snooze button. Hitting the snooze button can disrupt your sleep pattern, making it more challenging to get up in the future. It makes you feel you have the extra time to get the extra sleep you want when you don't.
- To help minimize the temptation to hit snooze, do not place your alarm clock next to the bed. It would help to move the alarm to the opposite side of the room, where you will be forced to "get up" to turn it off.
- Make up your bed as soon as you get out of it. Making up your bed right away makes it less appealing to crawl back into; plus, you

have started your day by accomplishing something immediately upon waking.

- As soon as you wake up, take a shower. The refreshing feeling from a warm or cold bath can invigorate you to get up and move.
- Exercise in the morning: Starting your day with exercise can boost your energy and motivation.
- Eat a healthy breakfast in the morning. I am a huge believer in not skipping breakfast. Breakfast does not need to be a heavy meal that may make you feel sluggish and exhausted; it is simply a nourishment to give you the energy to start your day. It can be as simple as fruit, yogurt, a bagel, or a couple of eggs.
- Create a morning routine that works for you. You may wish to read, pray, study, take a walk, or meditate. Mornings can become a time you look forward to doing something for yourself before the world has a chance to distract you from those things.

It can take a few weeks for your body to adjust, but be patient with yourself and persist in becoming the morning person you need to be to get to school on time. An earlier start can lead to other benefits like less traffic on your commute and a less stressful, less rushed start to your day.

Chapter 3

The Unexpected Dream Killers

Dream killers are the people in your life who you'd expect to be your biggest supporters, yet turn out to be the people who make your journey most difficult. What's worse is that they can be those closest to you. I have witnessed dream killers who were the student's parents, children, siblings, bosses, boyfriends/girlfriends, spouses, cousins, aunts/uncles, and even best friends. You'd think these individuals would do everything possible to help the student reach their goals. However, dream killers allow feelings of jealousy, insensitivity, envy, insecurity, and pettiness to overshadow the thoughts of helping the student succeed.

Dream killers are like the crabs in a bucket, who, instead of allowing one of their own to escape and succeed, pull them back down into collective misery. They're the naysayers, the ones who can't see the vision you're so passionate about, or worse, they see it but don't want you to achieve it because it reflects on their insecurities or unfulfilled ambitions.

When you're striving for a goal, you're vulnerable. You're putting yourself out there, taking risks, and often stepping out of your comfort zone. You need a support system, a group of cheerleaders who believe in you, even when you might start doubting yourself. Dream killers are the villains of this support system. They can erode your confidence with their negativity, plant seeds of doubt with their skepticism, and drain your energy with their pessimism.

The shocking part is that these dream killers often wear the masks of friends, family, or loved ones. They're the people you'd least expect to undermine your aspirations. It's one thing to face opposition from strangers or competitors; it's an entirely different emotional battlefield when the resistance comes from those you trust and care for.

Their detrimental impact can't be overstated. They might discourage you from taking opportunities, mock your ideas, or convince you that your dreams are unrealistic. They might even make you feel guilty for pursuing your ambitions, suggesting you're selfish or impractical.

In a way, dream killers steal a piece of your future every time they dissuade you from following your path. They might not do it maliciously – often, their actions are driven by their fears and issues – but the result is the same: a dream deferred, diminished, or even abandoned.

To safeguard your dreams, it's crucial to recognize these individuals and understand their potential impact on your goals. Surround yourself with people who inspire and encourage you, seek mentors who have achieved what you aspire to, and build a network of positivity that can withstand the weight of others' doubts and insecurities. Remember, your goals are your own, and while it's painful to acknowledge that not everyone will be your ally, it's empowering to take charge of your journey and choose who gets a seat on your bandwagon.

They Can Create Stumbling Blocks on Your Path

One student immediately comes to mind. Marlene was from Haiti had a home-based business as a baker. She did well and made good money baking and selling fresh bread and sweet cakes. She loved to cook but was limited to cooking dishes representing her culture, so she wanted to get her diploma in the U.S. and go to culinary school to learn to cook other types of cuisine. Marlene's longtime boyfriend and father of her daughter was not pleased with her decision to return to school and told her to quit. When she refused, he began doing things that made attending class difficult.

Initially, he started by creating arguments about simple things that would delay her getting to school on time. Eventually, he told her she should focus on baking and making money at home. He pointed out that since she started school, she was baking less and making less money for the household. To remedy the situation, Marlene began baking even earlier to ensure she produced the same as before. She mentioned that her boyfriend did not work; however, he began to take their only car in the mornings, leaving her without transportation. His actions affected her and their daughter's getting to school on time, so Marlene would have to pay for an Uber to drop them both at school. She could not afford to do that every day, so she transferred from my classes during the day to another teacher's class at night.

Her boyfriend made that transition difficult because he refused to watch their daughter in the evenings while she went to school. Some weeks later, she visited me with the biggest tears in her eyes to tell me she had to quit school because no matter what she tried, the lack of support at home was just too much of a struggle. My heart broke for her, so I encouraged her to do school online so she could continue to study when it was most convenient. The obstacle was that she didn't have a computer, so I told her to get a library card, borrow a tablet from her local library, and not allow anyone to kill her dreams of becoming the culinary artist she saw herself becoming.

A year later, she revisited me, with the biggest smile, to tell me that she told her boyfriend she'd leave him if he continued to get in her way, and she had passed three of her four subject tests. She aimed to start our tech college's culinary program in the fall. I was amazed because she looked completely different. Marlene no longer had the dark circular bags beneath her eyes from exhaustion and appeared invigorated and enthusiastic. I was impressed and proud that she had taken her destiny by the horns.

There was another woman whose boyfriend told her to her face that she was too old and too stupid to go back to school. He was physically and verbally abusive and told her to stop going because he was convinced she had a boyfriend on campus. When I asked why she put up with the abuse, she said it was because he paid all the household expenses. I explained that she had options to get away from her toxic situation. Unfortunately, she did stop coming to school.

Don't think boyfriends are the only ones who can make going to school difficult. Girlfriends can become an issue, too. I had a twenty-something-year-old student named Dante who, let's just say, was into corner pharmaceuticals. He was savvy and energetic but had difficulty getting a nine-to-five job due to his arrest record. He told me of many occasions where he was either stabbed, robbed, or beaten up because of his occupation. Dante had these grand ideas of businesses he wanted to start for himself, so he decided to get his diploma and continue towards a business degree. Despite wanting to turn his life around into one his grandma, who raised him, could be proud of, his girlfriend told him he was dumb for wanting to walk away from the fast money. Dante always gave her the funds to care for her hair, nails, and clothing. Unfortunately for her, the more hours Dante spent at school, the less time he had to hustle to make that cash.

Just as Dante planned to break up, he learned she was pregnant. He felt torn because he desired to provide a life for his new baby that he never had growing up, but he was tired of doing what he did to make money.

One day after class, he asked for my honest advice, so I asked him how much he needed to have stockpiled to leave "the pharmaceutical" industry. He said, "20 stacks". Then, I asked him how long he thought it would take to make that amount. He estimated it would take approximately one year, so I walked over to my whiteboard and did the math as he watched. I divided that twenty-thousand-dollar goal into 52 weeks (1 year) and then divided it again by a 40-hour work week.

The final calculations showed he would work for a little more than $7 an hour. I asked him how much risk he was willing to take for $7, plus the cost of looking over his shoulder every minute. He stared at me, shocked, and said, "Dang, Ms. Kydd, why did you have to break it down like that?" He said he never did the math, but it made him mad once he saw the numbers. He couldn't believe how little he was actually making. Just to drive the point home, I told him he needed to fire his boss because he was making less than minimum wage. We laughed, but he understood.

While significant others can create stumbling blocks, so can your children, specifically the grown-up ones. A case in point is when Maura started my class early one Monday morning. She was nervous about returning to school in her 50s. Still, she was so happy about being back in a classroom and the prospect of having classmates and focusing her energy on getting her credentials.

She walked up and spoke to me privately to express that it had been over 30 years since she had stepped foot in a classroom and to excuse her if she was too slow for the class. I reassured her that she was in the right place at the right time and would be just fine. I asked the others to welcome Maura to the family, so everyone immediately came over, said hello, and told her to sit wherever she liked. Her sigh of relief was apparent, but before the class ended, her cell phone rang. The first time, she simply swiped left to silence the call. A few minutes later, it rang again. She apologized and excused herself from the room. She returned annoyed but regrettably had to leave to pick up her daughter from work. The next day, she returned with the same enthusiasm, ready to try again. The phone rang, but this time, she turned it off. The following day was the same as before, but she answered the calls. She quickly apologized but needed to leave early and did not attend class until the following week.

Her initial enthusiasm was replaced with frustration because her daughter left her grandchild alone without asking her permission first. Without a word, Maura's daughter would leave the baby for days, keeping Maura stuck at home caring for the child. When she came back to school, she was so sad that she was already missing so many classes. She asked for any makeup work and explained that her daughter often left the baby at her house without her approval for days at a time, refused to give her help around the house, and was angry that Maura didn't like the baby's father, who encouraged the bad behavior. Maura was torn between making her daughter leave or allowing her to stay longer to get on her feet. While the student desperately wanted to be in class, she knew her daughter would continue to be a stumbling block. She allowed her daughter to remain in her home, which meant school was put on the back burner again.

Learn to Inspire Yourself, Because No One Else May Do It.

You must learn to be self-motivated despite the stumbling blocks placed in your way, especially when you have dream killers. You must constantly remind yourself why you are on this road to getting smarter and educating yourself. For some, making more money is enough inspiration to stick with this path. For others, money is not a good enough reason, so looking beyond the financial benefit to why you NEED the money or want higher education can encourage folks to do what may sometimes feel impossible. For example, I *need* money to provide my children with a stable and comfortable home. For you, it may be the *need* to purchase a better place to stay. It could be the *need* to pay medical bills for a loved one, start a business, save for a wedding, or do things that financial stability can bring. You must keep telling yourself there is a reward at the end of this decision to learn more and elevate your life. You are wiser than before if nothing else, and no one can take that away.

School can be challenging at times. Here are some tips for staying motivated:

- Set Clear Goals: Identify what you want to achieve, whether it's academic success, personal growth, or extracurricular accomplishments.
- Break Tasks into Smaller Steps: Divide larger projects or assignments into smaller, more manageable tasks to avoid feeling overwhelmed. For instance, instead of taking four classes, take only two.
- Celebrate Small Victories: Reward yourself for completing tasks or reaching benchmarks. The rewards you give yourself can vary depending on how big a milestone you must overcome. It could be as simple as going out for ice cream or treating yourself to a movie.
- Find your "Why": Connect what you learn in school to your passions and future goals. Let's say you always wanted to become a nurse and help save lives. Finishing school will help you obtain the credentials needed to work in that field and fulfill your passion, or it may also help you get a promotion to do more in that profession.
- Create a Study Routine: Establish a regular schedule to stay on track and avoid procrastination.
- Ask For Help When Needed: Don't hesitate to ask for assistance. Surround yourself with supportive peers, teachers, or mentors who encourage and inspire you.
- Find Your Balance: Create a weekly schedule that balances your job, schoolwork, relaxation time, and fun activities to avoid burnout.
- Stay Organized: Use tools like planners, calendars, or apps to stay on top of assignments and deadlines.
- Practice Self-Care: Prioritize your physical and mental well-being by getting enough sleep, exercising, and developing healthy habits.

Remember, motivation is a personal and ongoing process. Find what works best for you and stay committed to your goals.

Chapter 4

You Can Carry Anything with Support

Dream killers exist, but so do friends, family, co-workers, teachers, advisors, and others who will have your back during this endeavor. Depending on what you are trying to accomplish, it can take a tribe of people to make your goal successful. These *dream supporters* will be there to cheer you on and aid you from time to time.

I must use myself as an example here. My parents have been my biggest supporters in absolutely everything I have put my hands to do in life. I can't think of a time when they were not there- that moment doesn't exist. They are there physically and financially to back up my ideas. They step in to provide resources without being asked to do so, even for my students. So many of my students have met my parents because they often attend school events that I've coordinated, usually with food in hand. Back in elementary school, we had class grandmas who volunteered to help the teachers and hugged the kids who were having a bad day. With that in mind, I would consider my mom and dad "class parents." They have even mentored lots of my students, both my past middle school and adult students, whom they noticed had a spark or appeared discouraged and needed a loving hug and encouraging word. So, I know how special it is to have folks in your corner.

Appreciate your "Dream Supporters"

As a student, there will be days when you will be tired and tempted to give up, but your tribe will be there to say, "No, keep going. You got this." It is crucial that you always express your appreciation to them and not abuse the support they give.

For example, Alisa and her mom came to my class on Alisa's first day so that Mom could introduce herself and let me know to inform her if Alisa needed anything. The mother was friendly and reassured Alisa that she would provide the resources necessary to graduate. However, the daughter's response was insulting and downright embarrassing. Alisa turned to her mother and scolded her for, as she put it, always trying to ride her back. Her tone, body language, and words were harsh and unappreciative.

I was shocked that she would humiliate her mother in front of me, a stranger at this point. While I didn't know their history, the moment shook me to my core and did not sit well with me.

I turned to Alisa and said, "Excuse me, but that was not kind, and your behavior toward your mother is beyond disrespectful." I explained to her how much she would need her mom's help along the way, especially since she did not work to have the funds to pay for registration, supplies, exams, or transportation. It was wrong for her to shame her mother before strangers. I informed her that I would not tolerate rude behavior because we are family in my class. I asked her to apologize to her mom and said we would move forward and not mention it again. She hesitated, but after hearing the seriousness in my tone and seeing the seriousness in my eyes, she complied. The mom didn't say a word, but her eyes told me, "Thank you."

By the cold reaction I got from her in class that day, I could tell I had landed myself at the top of her "don't like" list, but I was okay with that because right is right.

After a few conversations with the young lady, I learned that she had gotten associated with the wrong crowd in high school and had gotten into fights many times. Her mother felt it best to remove her from the environment and crowd. She explained that she didn't mean to disrespect her mom but was angry that she was cut off from her friends and old school. I told her that jail would have done the same thing but with a much worse outcome. She looked at me and said, "That's true." I told her that her life's journey would include people who couldn't go everywhere she was meant to go and that sometimes it is best to leave certain people behind so she can elevate to the next level.

I noticed some sketches in her notebook (they were excellent), so I told her to think about where she would be if she were still enrolled in her old school. I asked her to illustrate her outcome if she was doing the same things she was engaged in while there. The next day, she brought a drawing of her in jail on one side and her in the hospital on the other. I asked her to explain how she came to that conclusion. By the end of her analysis, we were both crying and hugging it out. At that moment, her anger broke, her entire demeanor changed, and she became motivated to turn it all around.

In the end, Alisa bought her mother a massive bouquet, and presented it to her Mom at the graduation ceremony to show her appreciation for her unwavering support. By that point, she understood what I meant about how vital her mom's aid would be in getting to walk the stage. She even posted me on her social media page as her #favoriteteacherever. That was an honor.

Spouses and Children Can Be a Substantial Motivating Factor

I love putting stickers on assignments that scored mastery (75% or higher). It may sound funny, but adult students get excited to see a sticker on their papers! I even give certificates if they win class competitions. Many parents take pride in showing off their stickers and certificates to their kids. One student told me her daughter expected her to bring home an assignment that earned a sticker every day to prove she was doing her best in school. So, she knew she would have some explaining to do to her daughter on days the mom did not earn a sticker, so she would work diligently to earn her "sticker of honor" daily.

That, right there, is the root of having a mindset of excellence. It's reaching a certain threshold, striving to either maintain it or go beyond it, and putting in more effort if you fall short of that benchmark.

Sometimes, I Must Pull Out the Big Guns

I had another student who was very nervous about going back to school. Diane was a housewife for many years, but her children were older and in college. She said her husband had talked her into registering for class and believed it was her time to go back and pursue her nursing dreams. While she liked the sound of the idea, her confidence in herself was low. Diane was terrified of leaving her capacity as a housewife and doing things like going to school and the workforce after so many years. She was progressing well, so I told her I wanted her to take the test. She said, "No, I don't think I'm ready." I accepted that story for a few more weeks, but then I saw the need to pull out the big guns.

Her husband stopped by to pick her up one day and told me how his wife talks about me at home. I looked at him and saw my chance to rally his help. I told him I felt his wife would do well on the test and asked him to encourage her to go for it. He looked at his wife and said, "See, Honey, I told you, you are very smart!" He continued to say that if she took the test, pass or not, he would reward her with the mixer she had been eying in the store. She turned to me and said, "Ok".

I helped her schedule the test, and she passed it on her first attempt. She was overjoyed, and her confidence went through the roof. She told me she had scheduled her next subject test the following week. I didn't even have to appeal to her to test anymore because she saw the light at the end of the tunnel and was now running towards it on her own. By the end, her husband had bought her the mixer, the matching toaster, and the blender as a reward for such a job well done. Her children were proud of her success as well, and I enjoyed meeting them all at her graduation ceremony.

Chapter 5

How to Get Better with a Non-Traditional Education

Not all learning takes place in a classroom. While the focus of this book is to encourage people to go back to school and get at least the foundational knowledge of a high school diploma, I would hate to neglect to address the importance of other forms of education that can lead to a better life. Brick-and-mortar classrooms are not your only option to gain more knowledge. Just to define what a non-traditional education is, it's learning that takes place outside of a formal college, university, or trade school.

I am a huge advocate of being a life-long learner. Many of the credentials I hold were not obtained in a four-walled classroom. I have multiple certifications through online methods. As a matter of fact, I don't think I would have been able to earn my master's degree had it not been for me having access to the curriculum online during times that worked around my jam-packed daily schedule.

Advancing your life through non-traditional means is like taking the road less traveled to reach the same destination – success and personal growth. It's about leveraging the wealth of knowledge and skills that aren't confined to the four walls of a classroom.

You Can Harness the Power

You can harness the power of unconventional learning to propel yourself forward in many ways. First, the internet has made access to information so convenient and affordable. Platforms like Grow with Google, Coursera, Udemy, Study.com, and Khan Academy offer courses on everything from quantum physics to digital marketing. Don't get me started on YouTube. What can you learn on YouTube? Everything! These online resources allow you to tailor instruction to your interests and career goals. You can learn at your own pace, on your schedule, and often for a fraction of the cost of traditional schooling. This self-directed learning makes you knowledgeable and shows potential employers you're motivated and capable of taking the initiative.

To seize opportunities like these, you need to have some foundation in digital literacy. I can't express enough the importance of having technology skills, especially post-COVID. Every career path and industry use technology to advance and function.

One of my digital literacy class students worked in her desired field. She had all the mandated certifications required for the profession; however, her lack of computer skills made it difficult for her to hold on to the employment opportunity. The loss of that position fueled her to enroll in my course. If you are not tech-savvy, take the time to get some tips on how to use it. It might be as simple as asking the kids in your family how to do something. Kids these days are technology gurus.

You will need access to a desktop computer, laptop, tablet, or cell phone. Plus, you need a reliable internet connection. Suppose you do not have these tools readily available. In that case, you can visit your local library to gain free access with your library card. Most libraries offer computer classes and tutoring as well.

Other great non-traditional opportunities are apprenticeships and on-the-job training. Apprenticeships and on-the-job training can be a goldmine for practical experience. They throw you into the deep end and force you to swim, which can be a more effective teacher than theoretical knowledge. By working alongside experienced professionals, you can learn the processes of a trade or profession that aren't captured in textbooks. This type of hands-on learning can make you highly skilled and incredibly valuable in the job market.

Social networking is another powerful tool. Networking is a dynamic way to learn because it connects you with individuals who have diverse experiences and expertise. Engaging with a broad range of professionals exposes you to new ideas, perspectives, and knowledge you might not encounter in a traditional educational setting. Conversations allow you to gain insights into industry trends, best practices, and innovative solutions to problems.

It's a form of social learning where the exchange of information happens organically, often leading to mentorship opportunities. By building a robust professional network, you can access a collective intelligence that can guide you, offer advice, and present new learning pathways you might not have found on your own.

Travis, an adult culinary student with a passion for fusion cuisine, knew that to excel in the culinary world, he needed more than just technical skills; he needed a community and a taste of diverse culinary cultures. He turned to social media, joining niche foodie groups and following influential chefs on platforms like Instagram and Twitter. By engaging with posts, sharing his food creations, and asking for feedback, Travis gained valuable culinary tips. He caught the eye of a local restaurant owner who admired his unique style. She reached out to him through direct messaging and, after a few exchanges, offered him a chance to intern at her restaurant. This opportunity allowed Travis to work alongside seasoned chefs, learn the intricacies of restaurant management, and experiment with creating his recipes. Social networking expanded Travis's culinary knowledge and opened the door to hands-on experience and potential career advancement in the industry.

Remember that education is a vast, open field ripe for exploration through every tool and technology at our disposal. Whether through online courses, apprenticeships, or the vibrant world of social networking, each step is a stride toward personal and professional enrichment. Embrace the unconventional, for it is there that we often find the seeds of innovation and the roots of expertise. As you venture forth, remember that education is not just about gathering facts; it's about the connections we forge, the experiences we gain, and the horizons we expand. Be curious, be bold, and let the world be your classroom.

Chapter 6

Winners Without a Degree

I have a quote hanging above my classroom's entryway that says, "Education is what one has remembered *after they* left school," by Albert Einstein. Getting your high school diploma or degree can be like a doorway to endless possibilities; however, what makes a person a winner is their persistence in educating themselves by any means necessary to achieve their goals. Author, minister, and motivational speaker Rick Rigsby stated the wisest person he had ever met was a third-grade dropout. Rigsby proclaimed, "The words' dropout' and 'wisest person' in the same sentence are among the biggest oxymorons." Despite the contrasting statement, his third-grade dropout father had taught him some of the most profound pearls of wisdom.

Success Without School?

As I mentioned before, you do not have to have a traditional post-secondary education to become a mighty success. Whether your knowledge comes through conventional means, a non-traditional pathway, or, as Jay-Z calls it, "The school of hard knocks," learning what you need to know through whatever format you choose can put you on the road toward the career of your dreams.

Can you really have a great career without finishing a traditional high school? Certainly! Some well-known individuals who left high school before graduation and obtained their GED® diplomas include:

Jim Carrey and Michael J. Fox are two prominent examples of

individuals who did not traditionally complete their high school education but later achieved significant success in their respective fields. Jim Carrey left high school at 16 to assist his family financially despite maintaining excellent grades and being known for his comedic talent. He initially worked in security and maintenance roles before finding fame as a comedic actor.

Michael J. Fox also departed from high school, shy of graduating, to pursue acting opportunities in Hollywood. Despite facing personal and health challenges, he obtained his General Educational Development (GED®) credential at 34.

Numerous musicians, including Britney Spears, David Bowie, 50 Cent, Eminem, Pink, Jerry Garcia, and Waylon Jennings, have similarly foregone traditional high school education. Their careers in the music industry have flourished despite this non-traditional educational path.

In sports, Olympic gymnast Mary Lou Retton, professional boxer Oscar De la Hoya, and soccer player Mario Torres have all earned their GED® diplomas, demonstrating that athletic success can be achieved alongside or following alternative educational routes.

Lastly, Peter Jennings, a renowned news anchor, is another individual who found professional success after obtaining his GED®. His career in journalism reached notable heights, illustrating that academic qualifications are not the sole determinant of one's professional trajectory.

Remember, success isn't limited by the path you take. Whether through traditional education or alternative routes, determination and hard work pave the way to achievement! There are countless accounts of people who did not get a degree to become world-renowned. Response.com's website lists some well-known individuals who did not receive a degree yet went on to become some of the most outstanding entrepreneurs of our day and age:

- Richard Branson, founder and Chairman of Virgin
- Walt Disney, Disney Corporation Founder
- Bill Gates, Microsoft Founder
- Michael Dell, founder of Dell, Inc.
- Mark Zuckerberg, founder of Facebook
- Mark Cuban, entrepreneur, television personality, and owner of the Dallas Mavericks NBA team
- Steve Jobs, co-founder of Apple

These trailblazers did not compile higher-level credentials such as master's or Ph.D. degrees to seize the moment and begin their businesses. Richard Branson struggled with dyslexia, a learning disability that affects the skills of reading, spelling, and writing. He struggled academically, yet his sense of drive compelled him to become a business owner. Walt Disney took art and photography classes in high school, but at age sixteen, Walt left school to join the army (which he was later rejected for being too young). The experience he gained in art classes and working as an ambulance driver fueled his creativity and grit.

During high school, Steve Jobs attended several after-school lectures at Hewlett Packard. He went on to college but left after only one semester. That exposure to the tech world and his job as a game designer for Atari fueled his experience in the digital world. Mark Zuckerberg was enrolled in Harvard when he built Facebook with his roommates. He left Harvard to focus on building the online platform, but who would ever leave Harvard? He did and is now one of the youngest billionaires in the world. They all left those institutions to create companies that made them millionaires and billionaires.

I am not trying to convince you to leave your school to become the next super famous entrepreneur; what I am leading you to is that it is not only degree-holders who become successful. It is those who allow their desire to attain more and the work ethic to follow through with every experience and opportunity around them to gain the knowledge and insight to make their dreams a reality. If they can do it, you can, too, no matter your educational level. Learn from the people around you and by any means necessary. It would be best to have grit and believe in your purpose to excel.

The traditional path of completing formal education is often seen as a stepping stone to success. Still, it is by no means the only route. Many individuals have carved out prosperous careers and contributed significantly to various fields without the benefit of a completed degree. Success without formal education often hinges on self-directed learning, practical experience, and the tenacity to pursue one's passions against conventional norms. People like Steve Jobs and Bill Gates, who did not finish their higher education are testaments to the fact that success is not exclusively the domain of the traditionally schooled.

The Spirit of an Entrepreneur

Specific skills and attributes become more critical to thrive without a formal degree. The entrepreneurial spirit is often at the forefront, characterized by the ability to identify opportunities and the courage to take calculated risks. Self-taught individuals must possess a strong work ethic and the discipline to set their curriculum and pace of learning. Networking also plays a key role; building relationships with mentors, industry professionals, and peers can open doors that degrees often do. Additionally, practical skills such as financial literacy, marketing, and sales are invaluable, as they directly contribute to the ability to start and sustain a business or career.

Moreover, adaptability and continuous learning are essential in an ever-evolving job market. Those without formal education must independently acquire new skills and knowledge, stay current with industry trends, and pivot when necessary. Once again, critical thinking and problem-solving skills are instrumental. They enable individuals to navigate complex situations and innovate without structured guidance. Finally, verbal and written communication is crucial for articulating ideas, marketing oneself, and collaborating. While a degree can open doors, these skills and qualities ultimately forge the path to success.

It has been said that some of the most successful people in the world are self-educated. "These are the people who are engaged, focused, and driven, and you'll find these people from all walks of life and with varying degrees of education. These are the people who learn to make a difference in the world – not necessarily pad their resumes with degrees and credentials. These people learn when they're not on a deadline or budget – they learn because they want to." (Response)

Chapter 7

Understanding and Harnessing Your Unique Learning Style

Before we dive into the details, let's understand the concept of learning styles. There are four commonly known learning styles: visual, which deals with learning through seeing; auditory, which means learning through listening; reading/writing style, which is the method of learning through reading and writing; and kinesthetic, which requires learning through doing and experiencing the content hands-on. These styles reflect how individuals absorb, process, and retain information. Discovering your learning style is the key to determining which strategy you should take to interact with new ideas and information.

Each of us possesses a learning style as unique as our fingerprint. By recognizing and comprehending these personal methods of processing information, we gain the power to unlock our full potential in acquiring knowledge.

For instance, I am a visual and kinesthetic learner. I must "see" and "do" it to make sense of new information. For example, if I must drive to a location I have never been to. In that case, a person cannot simply tell me (auditory) how to reach my destination. I need a tool like Google Maps, which shows me (visually) each turn and distance I must physically take (kinesthetic). As a result, I can return to that address without any future guidance. Since I know my learning style, I shouldn't ask someone to explain how to get where I need to go because hearing the directions will leave me just as confused as before. Instead, I know to ask the individual for the address, which I will input into the Google Maps app and allow it to "show" me the way.

The Great Discovery

Discovering your learning style can significantly enhance your educational experience and improve your ability to retain and apply information. For instance, when the instructor is teaching a new lesson, you can request they present the concept in your learning style to ensure you grasp the fundamentals. Here are some tips to help you identify your personal learning preferences:

- Reflect on Past Learning Experiences: Consider situations where you've learned effectively. What were the common elements? Did you benefit from discussions, hands-on activities, or visual aids? Think about when you felt most engaged and understood the material well. Were you reading a book, watching a video, or participating in a group activity? These instances can provide valuable insights into your preferred learning style. Try Different Methods: Experiment with various learning techniques, such as using flashcards, creating mind maps, participating in group discussions, or teaching concepts to others—notice which methods make learning more accessible and enjoyable for you.
- Take Learning Style Assessments: Complete online quizzes or questionnaires to identify learning styles. Learning style assessments are designed to help you know how you learn best and can provide a more comprehensive understanding of your learning style. If you are enrolled in school, your advisor may have one available. If not, you can find free resources online, such as *www.learningstylequiz.com.*
- Pay Attention to Your Senses: Observe which senses you rely on most when learning. Do you prefer to listen (auditory), watch (visual), or engage in physical activity (kinesthetic)?
- Consider Your Interests and Hobbies: Your hobbies and activities outside a formal learning environment can also hint at your

learning style. For example, you may be a kinesthetic learner if you enjoy crafts or building models.

- Analyze Your Note-Taking Habits: Look at how you take notes during lectures or reading. Do you write down everything, draw diagrams, or record the lecture to listen to it again?

- Evaluate Your Concentration: Notice when and where you concentrate best. Is it while listening to music, in a quiet room, or when you're moving around?

- Seek Feedback: Ask teachers, tutors, or peers how you learn and effectively engage with the material.

- Monitor Your Energy Levels: Pay attention to when you feel most energetic and engaged during the learning process. This can indicate the types of activities that suit your learning style.

- Be Open to Combining Styles: Recognize that you might not fit perfectly into one category and that combining elements from different learning styles could be the most effective approach for you. For example, if you are a visual learner, you can enhance your learning by incorporating kinesthetic elements, such as drawing diagrams or using physical objects to represent concepts. This way, you can make your learning experience more engaging and effective. Remember, learning styles are not one-size-fits-all, and they can evolve. It's essential to remain flexible and adapt your learning strategies as you discover what works best for you in different contexts.

The Struggle is Real

Let's look at this scenario with Michael, a diligent adult student who returned to college to complete his degree. Despite his dedication and hard work, he struggled to keep up with his peers. Michael attended every class, took ample notes, and spent long hours studying. Still, when it came to exams and assignments, his performance failed to reflect the effort he was putting in.

Confused and disheartened, Michael began to question his ability to succeed academically. He noticed that while he could easily engage in discussions and clearly articulate his thoughts verbally, the traditional methods of studying through reading and writing needed to be revised. This disconnect made studying tedious and ineffective.

One day, Michael decided to seek advice from his academic advisor. During their meeting, the advisor listened to Michael's concerns and suggested he might benefit from exploring different learning styles to find one that suited him best.

She explained that people have diverse ways of processing information. Some are visual, grasping concepts better through images. Other students are auditory and benefit from listening and speaking. Yet, kinesthetic learners must engage in physical activity or hands-on experiences to fully understand new information.

Intrigued by this insight, Michael agreed to try out various learning techniques. He began by joining a study group, where he could discuss and debate topics, which catered to his strength in verbal communication. He also started to use educational podcasts, audiobooks, and YouTube, allowing him to absorb information through listening, which he found more natural and effective.

Furthermore, Michael incorporated more active learning methods into his routine. He used flashcards to visualize essential concepts and created diagrams to map out ideas. During his study sessions, Michael would often gesture to help cement the information in his mind. As Michael adapted to these new strategies, he noticed a significant improvement in his comprehension and retention of the material. He became more engaged in his studies and found that he could recall information more quickly and apply it more easily.

The revelation of his auditory and kinesthetic learning preferences was a pivotal moment for Michael. With this newfound understanding of his learning style, he could adapt his study habits accordingly. This clarity and relief led to improved grades, boosted confidence, and a renewed sense of optimism in pursuing his academic goals. Michael's experience taught him an invaluable lesson: embracing one's unique learning style makes the path to educational success more apparent and attainable.

Chapter 8

Bridging the Gap: The Power of ESOL

ESOL stands for English Speakers of Other Languages. Each year, hundreds of thousands of people migrate to countries where English is the primary language spoken. According to KFF, "Most immigrants – regardless of where they came from or how long they've been in the U.S. – say they came for more opportunities for themselves and their children." Learning English is usually near the top of the list of priorities, alongside gaining housing and employment.

Earning an ESOL qualification demonstrates that you have good speaking, writing, listening, and reading skills in English. This credential will help improve your social interactions and everyday life, and is also a great way to show employers your language skills.

"Despite an improved situation relative to their countries of birth, many immigrants report facing serious challenges, including high levels of workplace and other discrimination, difficulties making ends meet, and confusion and fears related to U.S. laws and immigration policies." (KFF) In today's globalized world, where boundaries are increasingly blurred, the ability to communicate effectively in English has become more than just a beneficial skill—it's a necessity. ESOL programs serve as a critical bridge, connecting non-native speakers to a world of otherwise inaccessible opportunities.

The Professional Edge

For adults, ESOL represents more than just language proficiency; it's a tool that can reshape their professional landscape. In competitive job markets, having a solid command of English can help an employer decide between two candidates. ESOL qualifications are not just about language; they are about empowerment and enabling individuals to participate fully in all aspects of life in English-speaking countries.

I've said it before. The resume may get you the interview, but the interview gets you the job. An applicant who can communicate with confidence is something employers seek. Indeed, mastering English through ESOL courses can be a transformative experience for adults. It's like acquiring a key to a vast library of opportunities; each new word and phrase unlocks potential job offers, collaborations, and social connections. In industries where jargon and clear communication are pivotal, fluency in English is not just preferred—it's essential. *Being multilingual is a huge asset in the workplace.* ESOL graduates often stand out in a pile of applications to hiring managers who value effective communication across multiple languages.

A Story of Exclusion

Consider Maria, a skilled worker from Colombia, who was disadvantaged in her workplace due to her limited English proficiency. Despite her expertise in the field, her ideas were often overlooked in meetings, and she missed out on promotions because she couldn't express herself as effectively as her English-speaking peers. This treatment not only affected her career growth but also her self-esteem.

Maria's story is familiar, echoing the struggles of many non-native English speakers in the global workplace. She realized that she needed to take action to break through the invisible barrier that language had created. Determined to turn her situation around, Maria enrolled in an English language course after work. Juggling her job, studies, and personal life was a challenge, but the promise of a brighter future fueled her.

As the weeks turned into months, Maria's colleagues noticed a change. Her contributions to meetings became more frequent, and her confidence grew. She started to voice her opinions more clearly, and her ideas were met with the recognition they deserved. Her improved language skills also allowed her to understand the nuances of workplace culture better, helping her to navigate office dynamics more effectively. Maria even became more comfortable talking with co-workers during lunchtime.

Maria's efforts were noticed by her superiors, so when a leadership position opened, her name was near the top of the list. Maria's unique perspective as a skilled worker who had overcome language barriers added to her appeal as a candidate. She was proficient in her job and embodied the resilience and determination the company valued.

The day Maria was promoted was a significant milestone in her life. It was a testament to her hard work and the importance of effective communication on the job. She became an inspiration to her colleagues, especially those facing similar challenges. Maria's story reminds us that while language can be a barrier, it can also be a bridge to new opportunities and personal growth.

Language Can Help Expand a Business

I needed to have a glass door repaired for my shower. I used an online search engine and found a company located in the next county, Miami Dade. Through the search engine, I was able to make an appointment for the repair without ever meeting the service technician who owned the company.

Miami is known for its vast Latino population, so this owner only had Hispanic clients. When the gentleman arrived at my home, he was punctual and very friendly, but the problem was that he only spoke Spanish, and I only speak English. My shower door is enormous since it is wide and nearly reaches the bathroom ceiling. The hinges needed to be replaced, and he had no employees to help him fix it, so he needed my assistance. This door was extremely heavy and needed to be held steady while he removed and replaced the hinges. I had no clue what he was instructing me to do to keep from crushing his fingers in the hinges or causing us to drop the door, which would've been dangerous for us both. I tried to use Google Translate, but we needed to have our hands free to switch back and forth between the languages. It was tough, but through non-verbal cues, we figured it out.

Once we reached the part that no longer required my assistance, he finished the job and thanked me profusely. Because I was his assistant, he gave me a great discount! I gave him my school business card and told him to email me so I could help him register for ESOL classes. I believe that if he learned English, he could grow his business beyond the Miami area into counties further north, where new construction is booming.

From Success to Starting Over

Then there's the story of Ahmed, a successful business owner from the Middle East. Back home, he was well-respected, and his enterprise thrived. However, he faced a harsh reality upon moving to the United States. His lack of English proficiency meant starting from scratch—his language barrier overshadowed his business expertise.

Undeterred, Ahmed enrolled in an ESOL course. The journey was challenging, but he was determined to regain his independence. As his English improved, so did his prospects. He began networking and understanding the local market and eventually launched a new business. This time, he was equipped with the language skills to navigate the American business landscape successfully.

I once heard about a student named Diego, a janitor for a family-owned store. His employers treated him with little respect because they assumed that his quiet nature meant he was of low intelligence. One day, a customer walked into the store and greeted him upon seeing Diego, saying, "How are you, Dr. Acosta?" Diego's employer asked the woman how she knew Diego. She informed them that Diego was a highly sought-after dentist in their community in their country. The employer was surprised to discover Diego's impressive qualifications and standing. They treated him according to what they perceived as his having low intelligence and capabilities, which were influenced by his reserved demeanor at work. However, Diego was quite talkative. His apparent shyness with his bosses stemmed from his difficulty in expressing himself fluently in English, leading him to speak less.

Ahmed and Diego are like many others who move to a new country and then must begin their careers from scratch. They might have been doctors, business owners, government workers, or paraprofessionals back home. Yet, they often can't continue their careers immediately once they move. Picture being a doctor for years, then moving somewhere new and having to learn the language first so that you can go back to school and earn your medical degree all over again.

The Social Fabric

Beyond the workplace, ESOL is crucial for social integration. It allows adults to participate fully in their communities, from conversing with neighbors to understanding cultural norms. This social aspect is vital for building a sense of belonging and fostering mutual understanding in diverse societies. For instance, when adults learn English, they can converse with people who live near them. These conversations help them make friends and feel like they are part of the neighborhood. Learning English also helps people understand the culture in their new home. They can learn about local traditions, holidays, and ways of life, which makes it easier for them to fit in.

Knowing English helps adults get access to essential services like healthcare and banking. They can also communicate with other people they will encounter daily like strangers, co-workers, store clerks, etc. without a translator. This skill is helpful because life in a new country can be challenging, and talking to people who provide services and benefits helps them learn how to use these services and make good choices for their families.

When people learn a new language, they often feel more confident. This confidence can help them try new things and meet new people. Speaking a common language helps everyone understand each other better in places with many different cultures. This can reduce misunderstandings and make the community stronger.

Overall, ESOL helps people who speak other languages become active in their new communities. It assists non-English speakers in becoming involved members of their new home, simplifies their everyday lives, and helps them form relationships with others.

Enriching Family Life

ESOL skills are invaluable for parents. They enable them to engage with their children's education, communicate with teachers, and help with homework. This involvement is crucial for their children's academic success and a solid family unit.

Understanding and speaking English opens a world of opportunities for parents. It's like a key to a secret garden where every conversation with their child's teacher blossoms into a partnership that nurtures the child's educational journey. Picture the warmth in a parent's heart when they can decipher the stories their child tells about school, the pride that swells within when they can actively participate in parent-teacher conferences, and the joy that comes from being able to help with a tricky homework problem. These moments are more than just academic interactions; they're threads weaving a tighter bond within the family fabric.

Imagine the peace of mind that flows through a parent when they no longer feel sidelined by a language barrier. It's more than being able to communicate; it's about belonging and being part of a community. When parents can exchange a friendly chat at the school gates or offer suggestions during school meetings, they're improving their self-esteem and setting an example for their children. When I taught at the middle school, I recall having a parent-teacher conference that included a mother and her son, my student. The mom spoke little English, so her son was our translator. I was suspicious that the student may not have been translating accurately because there were moments when I shared how low her son's grades had plummeted. Yet, the mother showed no change in emotion or expressed any concern. Once I asked a fellow teacher to translate, the mom reacted more like a parent shocked that her child was failing. The mom apologized and appreciated the notification of her son's progress and the advice to help him remediate his weak areas.

When parents go back to school to strengthen their English, it shows their kids the importance of perseverance and the value of education while reinforcing the idea that it's never too late to learn something new. This emotional empowerment is a silent motivator for the entire family, echoing in the conversations around the dinner table. ESOL is not just about immediate benefits; it's about lifelong learning and adaptation. The world is constantly evolving, and language skills need to keep pace. For adults, ESOL is a commitment to continuous improvement and personal growth.

An Opportunity of Hope

The impact of ESOL extends beyond the individual. As adults improve their language skills, they contribute to the economy, enrich the cultural tapestry, and enhance the collective knowledge base. ESOL graduates often become advocates and mentors, helping others navigate the challenges they once faced.

ESOL does more than help one person. When adults improve their English, they can do more in their jobs and add to the money the place makes. They also bring different traditions and ideas, making the place more exciting and innovative. People who finish ESOL classes sometimes help new people by sharing what they have learned and giving advice. They guide others through complicated situations like the ones they had before.

English is often referred to as the global language, and for good reason. It's the language of international business, science, technology, and diplomacy. ESOL opens doors to this global stage, allowing individuals to participate in conversations that shape our world. ESOL programs provide hope by offering opportunities for better education and jobs in an English-speaking world. For those who migrant to the U.S. or move from one state to another, being designated as a resident in your new home can reduce education costs significantly. To get the best tuition rate, a student must be classified as a resident within that state (check the guidelines for your area). There is usually a 3-step process:

- Dependency: Determine if you are classified as a dependent or independent
- Citizenship: Student must be a US citizen or eligible non-citizen
- Established residency: Person must provide proof of establishing and maintaining legal residency for at least 12 consecutive months *before* the start of classes

Embracing ESOL

ESOL should be embraced. For some people, it's like a safety rope that helps them not to fall. For others, it's a step they can climb to reach their goals. And for many, it's like the ground they stand on to build their lives. Adults who want to live and do well in places where people speak English need ESOL.

As a past ESOL Bridge teacher, I admit teaching this demographic of students was fantastic! They have such a genuine love and appreciation for their instructors. They often strive to give their best and don't take the efforts of their teachers in vain. The importance of ESOL cannot be overstated. It's a lifeline for many, a steppingstone for some, and a foundation for others. For adults seeking to navigate the complexities of life in an English-speaking environment, ESOL is not just important— it's essential. Through the stories of Maria and Ahmed, we see the transformative power of language education and the profound impact it can have on an individual's life and the community at large.

Chapter 9

Back-to-School Toolbox

Welcome to your Back-to-School Guide! This guide is designed to help you navigate your return to school successfully. Remember, your honest and thoughtful responses will be valuable tools in motivating and guiding you through your educational journey. The next pages will contain some tools to guide you as you *get back to school*.

- Goal Setting Guide
- How to Study Guide
- How to Create a Vision Board Guide
- Plan of Action Sheet
- Going Back to School Tip Sheet

Goal Setting Guide

What I want to achieve by going back to school and why.	
As a result of gaining my education, I will be able to...	
To succeed, I need to remove these barriers...	

To succeed, I need to add...	
I will commit to...	
I want to meet my goal by this date or time...	

How-to-Study Guide

Reduce Interference	Stay away from your bed Stay away from your phone Stay away from the television Do not turn on music (unless it aids in concentration)
Plan Your Schedule	It is important to plan your study schedule so you will know exactly what you need to do each day.
20-Minute Rule	Study for 20 minutes and take a break for 10 minutes. Research shows that the human attention span lasts 20 minutes. After that amount of time, remaining focused becomes more challenging.
Re-write What You've Learnt	By writing what you learnt again and again, you will internalize the concepts. This is an age-old strategy which is still very effective.
Use Funny Mnemonics to Remember	A mnemonic device is like a memory trick that helps you remember something easier. It could be a rhyme, a song, a phrase, or even an image. Basically, it's a fun way to turn something hard to remember into something easier by connecting it to something you already know or can easily remember. For example, to remember the colors of the rainbow (red, orange, yellow, green, blue, indigo, violet), you might use the mnemonic "Roy G. Biv," where each letter stands for the first letter of each color. Another famous mnemonic to remember the order of operations in math is "Please Excuse My Dear Aunt Sally" = parenthesis, exponents, multiplication, division, addition and subtraction. It's like a secret code for your brain to unlock memories!

Use Images to Explain Concepts	Images are very powerful tools. Our brains like images better than words. Thus, by translating a concept or topic into a picture, you are more likely to remember it.
Stay Positive	This is one of the most important items on this list. See mistakes as learning opportunities, so don't moan or complain. Don't tell yourself, "This is too hard" or "I will never understand". Don't get discouraged, because if you stick with it, you WILL succeed!
Go to Bed	Knowledge, comprehension, motor learning and everything else happens because of neural connections in the brain. When you're too tired, the rate of neural connections comes to a halt.

Vision Board Guide

Creating a vision board is a fun and creative way to visualize your goals and dreams. Here's a step-by-step guide to help you make your own:

1. Gather Your Materials:

- Poster board, corkboard, or any sturdy surface to serve as the base of your vision board.
- Magazines, newspapers, or printed images from the internet that contain pictures and words related to your goals and aspirations.
- Scissors, glue, tape, or pins to attach the images and words to your board.
- Markers, colored pencils, or pens to add your own drawings or writings.

2. Set Your Intentions:

- Take some time to reflect on your goals and dreams. What do you want to achieve or manifest in your life? Think about different areas such as career, relationships, health, personal growth, and hobbies.

- Write down your intentions or goals in a journal or piece of paper. Be specific and positive in your wording.
- Only include the things on your vision board that you are absolutely certain you want to achieve. *Do NOT* add something unless you are fully committed to making it happen.

3. Find Inspiration:

- Flip through magazines, newspapers, or online sources to find images and words that resonate with your intentions and goals. Look for pictures that evoke positive emotions and represent the life you envision for yourself.

4. Select Images and Words:

- Cut out or print the images and words that you want to include on your vision board. Choose a variety of visuals that inspire and motivate you.
- You can also include quotes, affirmations, or phrases that resonate with you and reinforce your goals.

5. Arrange and Decorate:

- Lay out your selected images and words on the base of your vision board. Experiment with different arrangements until you find a layout that feels right to you.
- Get creative! Use markers, stickers, glitter, or any other decorative materials to personalize your vision board and make it visually appealing.

6. Attach the Elements:

- Once you're happy with the layout, glue, tape, or pin each image and word onto your vision board. Make sure everything is securely attached.

7. Reflect and Visualize:

- Take a moment to step back and admire your completed vision board. Reflect on the goals and dreams it represents.
- Place your vision board in a prominent location where you'll see it every day, such as your bedroom wall or workspace.
- Spend a few minutes each day visualizing yourself achieving your goals and living the life you've envisioned while looking at your vision board.

8. Update and Revisit:

- Your vision board is a dynamic tool that can evolve over time as your goals change and you make progress toward achieving them.
- Regularly update your vision board by adding new images or words that align with your current aspirations.
- Take time to revisit your vision board periodically to stay inspired and focused on your dreams.

Creating a vision board is not only a fun activity but also a powerful tool for manifesting your goals and turning your dreams into reality. Enjoy the process and let your creativity flow!

Plan of Action

These are the action steps I need to take to go back to school...	
I will start and complete the action steps within this amount of time...	
These people may be my *dream killers*. I will avoid their negative behaviors by...	

These people are my *dream supporters*. They can help me by...	
Whenever I get discouraged or lose motivation, I will do this to get back on track...	

Going Back-to-School Tip Sheet

Here's a set of clear and easy-to-understand tips that can assist you in going back to school:

1. Getting Organized:

- Gather all necessary school supplies such as notebooks, pens, pencils, and textbooks.
- Set up a designated study area at home, free from distractions.
- Use a planner or calendar to note down important dates like exams, project deadlines, and extracurricular activities.
- Create a daily or weekly schedule that includes study time, breaks, and other commitments.
- Organize digital files and folders on your computer for easy access to class materials.

2. Time Management:

- Prioritize tasks by importance and deadline.
- Break down large projects or assignments into smaller, manageable tasks.
- Use a timer or app to help stay focused during study sessions.
- Allocate specific time blocks for studying, relaxation, exercise, and socializing.
- Regularly review and adjust your schedule to ensure balance and productivity.

3. Study Skills:

- Take effective notes during lectures or while reading textbooks.
- Use active learning techniques such as summarizing, questioning, and teaching the material to others.
- Practice self-testing through quizzes, flashcards, or practice problems.

- Find a study method that works best for you, whether it's visual, auditory, or kinesthetic learning.
- Seek help from teachers, tutors, or classmates if you're struggling with a particular subject.

4. Stress Management:

- Practice relaxation techniques like deep breathing, meditation, or yoga.
- Engage in regular physical activity to reduce stress and improve overall well-being.
- Maintain a healthy lifestyle by eating nutritious foods, getting enough sleep, and avoiding excessive caffeine or alcohol.
- Take breaks when needed and avoid overloading yourself with too many commitments.
- Talk to someone you trust if you're feeling overwhelmed or anxious about school.

5. Setting Goals:

- Identify short-term and long-term goals for the school year, both academic and personal.
- Make goals specific, measurable, achievable, relevant, and time-bound (SMART).
- Break down goals into smaller action steps and track your progress regularly.
- Celebrate achievements along the way to stay motivated and focused.
- Adjust goals as needed based on changing circumstances or priorities.

Section 2

The Superheroes

(The Adult Educators)

Chapter 10

The Other Superheroes

Teachers, in general, should be recognized for the valuable resource they are. If it were not for teachers, who could gain the foundation of knowledge needed to navigate the world? However, adult educators are often a precious commodity that is overlooked. As I quoted at the start of the book, "The best thing you can do for a child is teach their parents so they can provide more time and resources to their kids." Without the essential contribution of these educators, many adults would have fewer opportunities to learn in ways that will positively impact their lives, their families, and our economy.

Let's meet Ms. Carignan

Ms. Carignan is a beacon of inspiration in her classroom, and her motto is "Math is Lit." By day, she teaches Adult Basic Math and GED® math; by night, she's often found teaching lessons in math, science, social studies, and language that cater to the unique lives of additional GED® students at a different adult community school. These students juggle jobs, families, and the heavy weight of past educational failures. Yet, Ms. Carignan knows that beneath those layers of doubt, there's a spark waiting to be kindled.

One of her students, for instance, was a single mother of two who had dropped out of high school years ago. The thought of algebra sent shivers down her spine, but Ms. Carignan saw her potential. With patience that would make a saint nod in respect, she tutored the student, breaking down complex equations into bite-sized, understandable pieces. Under

Ms. Carignan's tutelage, the student conquered her fear of numbers and passed her GED® math test with flying colors to become a proud graduate. The student can now help her children with their homework, which is a secondary effect of Ms. Carignan's dedication. Now, the student's new motto is "Math is Lit!"

The Heart and Soul of Adult Educators

I have often heard it said, "Teaching is a work of heart." Being an adult educator is a role that carries with it a profound emotional depth, often unseen and underappreciated by those outside the educational arena. These teachers enter a world where their students' lives are interwoven with complications extending far beyond the classroom. The weight of this responsibility is immense, yet they embrace it with a steadfast dedication that is nothing short of heroic. Adult educators are not merely instructors; they are lifelines, confidants, and sometimes the only support in their students' turbulent worlds. Their ability to balance the demands of teaching with the emotional needs of their students is a testament to their incredible strength and compassion.

Adult educators bear a unique burden that is heavy with the knowledge of their students' complex situations. From financial hardships to personal struggles, these educators are privy to the stark realities that can hinder learning and growth. Yet, they do not shy away from these challenges. Instead, they seek ways to help, often going above and beyond their job descriptions to ensure each student has the support they need to succeed. Their commitment to their students' well-being is a remarkable display of empathy and concern that defines the very essence of their role.

Consider the scenario of a student who, against all odds, walks into the classroom with a history of homelessness, addiction, job discrimination, mental illness, educational defeat, life-altering medical conditions, abuse, or criminal records. Their life outside the school walls is a battle for survival, a daily confrontation with circumstances that would easily overwhelm the strongest of spirits. Yet, in the presence of an adult educator, this student finds an ally. The educator, recognizing the acute needs of their pupil, does not stop providing education. They become a bridge to a better life, connecting the student with essential services, counseling, and support networks. This level of involvement is far more than required, yet for the educator, it is a moral condition they cannot ignore.

The impact of such actions is monumental. Can you imagine trying to focus in school when you're not sure where you will sleep that night? For the student who has known the cold, hard ground as a bed and the shadows of abuse as their constant companions, the adult educator's intervention is life-changing. Access to services provides not just immediate relief but also a path forward, a chance to rebuild and reclaim a sense of stability over their life. This is the power of an adult educator's influence – the ability to alter the trajectory of a person's life through compassion, commitment, and the sheer force of will to make a difference.

Clark Kent has Nothing on these Undercover Heros

Just imagine that in hundreds of cities lies a wealth of knowledge, where dreams are reignited, and hope is as tangible as textbooks on desks. This is the realm of the adult educator, a true superhero in plain clothing whose superpower is the ability to change lives with nothing more than words, encouragement, and an unyielding belief in their students' potential.

Adult instructors give more than just their time; they provide pieces of their hearts. They stay late, arrive early, and reach into their pockets to provide supplies for their students. I have witnessed more times than I can count an adult ed. teacher buying a meal, a test prep book, a scientific calculator or a test for a student who did not have the means to afford it. When the student offers to repay the deed, the instructor says, "No, pay me back by getting your diploma."

They are counselors, cheerleaders, and sometimes the only source of positive reinforcement their students receive. With adult educators, students might be able to find the confidence to pursue their dreams. These teachers go above and beyond to ensure their students have the tools to thrive. Their sacrifices are many, from creating engaging lessons to providing emotional support to those in need.

Their classrooms are hallowed grounds where judgment is left at the door. Each desk is a testament to second chances. In this environment of unwavering support, learning is not just about academics; it's about growth, self-discovery, and breaking the chains of self-doubt. These facilitators create a space where it's okay to ask questions, make mistakes, and, most importantly, dream of a brighter future.

Adult educators may not wear capes but possess a hero's heart. They see the invisible potential in each person who walks through their door and works tirelessly to ensure that potential is realized. Their students may feel defeated by life's harsh lessons, but they leave with diplomas, certifications, and the knowledge that they have someone in their corner, cheering for them every step.

Where Would We be Without Them?

Imagine a world without adult educators, where classrooms lack the warmth and guidance these dedicated individuals bring. Grown-ups also need support at school, so with their teacher's caring heart and unwavering support, those students would feel safe, with a safe space to learn and grow. These educators are like anchors in a storm, providing stability and encouragement to those who may feel adrift or unsure of their path. They offer more than just lessons; they offer hope, belief, and a sense of belonging that is invaluable to students' well-being and success.

Many individuals could miss the opportunities and support needed to overcome life's challenges in a world without adult educators. These facilitators play a crucial role in shaping students' academic knowledge and self-confidence, resilience, and belief in their abilities. Their impact goes far beyond the classroom, reaching into the fabric of society and influencing the future of our communities.

The role of an adult educator demands recognition and respect. Their work is not simply a job; it is a calling that they answer with every fiber of their being. They are the unsung architects of second chances, the quiet warriors who fight for their students' futures. To all adult educators, your emotional investment and tireless efforts define what it means to serve others. Your actions embody humanity at its best; you deserve our deepest gratitude and highest praise.

Adult educators, you are the architects of dreams, the weavers of opportunity, and the quiet guardians of second chances. Your sacrifices do not go unnoticed, and your impact echoes through the lives of every student you inspire. Thank you for being incredible at changing lives, one lesson at a time. The patience and understanding you exhibit, the extra hours you invest, and the personal resources you often tap into, all in the name of supporting your students, are acts of kindness that resonate through the lives of those you teach. You are the unsung heroes who ignite hope and inspire change, fostering environments where learning becomes a gateway to personal growth and transformation. Your unwavering belief in your students' potential is a powerful force that empowers them to strive for better, even when the odds are stacked against them.

Chapter 11

The Ms. Kydd Approach

My journey as an educator started in 2005 when I joined the United States Peace Corps. I never imagined myself as a teacher, but my service catapulted me into the classroom when I became a manager and teacher of a community resource center in a small village in St. Vincent and the Grenadines *(I share more details of this in my other book, Don't Get Bitter, Get Better)*. While my degree was in Communications and Public Relations, the Minister of Telecommunications offered me a position as the community resource center manager. That new, two-story building included an office, library, dining hall, kitchen, and computer lab with 25 desktop computers. It resided at the top of a hill unopened for months prior to my arrival. I taught digital literacy and presentation skills classes for kids aged 5-8 and adults. I quickly realized that I didn't have the energy nor the patience to teach elementary kids, so I decided to focus on the adults. I salute you elementary teachers everywhere! Seeing a student's intellectual light bulb turn on because they learned something new was the best feeling. I realized back then that keeping students motivated was just as important as the content you taught. Without it, they could easily fall off track. I served for three years.

Once I returned to the U.S., I decided to continue teaching. I was a pool substitute with the Broward School District until I got a permanent position as a middle school language arts teacher at a charter school.

Platinum Club

I quickly became a very popular teacher among the students because I always incorporated lots of technology to teach and engage them. I pioneered various incentives to inspire students to strive for consistent growth and academic achievement. For example, I started what I called "Platinum Club Parties." I got the idea from Willy Wonka and the Chocolate Factory. However, instead of a golden ticket discovered by luck, it was a platinum ticket that had to be earned. This highly exclusive event occurred on a Friday after school at the end of each quarter for my students who either scored at high levels consistently throughout the term or significantly improved from the previous term. So, out of my 125 students, only 25-30 got a platinum club invitation. *I went all out.*

Students who met the criteria received a fancy, personalized silver invitation and parent permission slip to attend. Since the school had a strict uniform policy, the kids relished dressing casually for the event. My classroom was transformed with balloons, glittery decorations hanging from the ceiling, and silver tablecloths. There was loud party music (which is why it was always after school), food (usually hot dogs, pizza, chips, cupcakes, and drinks), lots of dancing, and freestyle rap battles. The event became so popular that I needed a bouncer at the door to keep outsiders from crashing the par-tay!

Students worked hard to earn an invitation, and once they did, they took great pride in showing it off, but held on tight not to lose it because no invitation meant no entry, *no exceptions!* I mandated this rule to teach them the importance of responsibility for their property. I truly enforced this when I turned away a student who did receive an invitation but lost it before the event. With a heavy heart, I told her she could not enter without the ticket. She cried, but you better believe she worked hard to earn one for the following term, and she kept that ticket under lock and key to never lose it again. When dealing with young people, you have to say what you mean and mean what you say.

At the end of the function, we always took a group photo so I could post the group's portrait on my "wall of fame" until the next celebration to motivate those who didn't get to attend. Those who managed to land on the wall of fame, took bragging rights to a whole new level. Parents, especially those who often had issues with their child being motivated at school, raved at how much of a boost in effort their kids had while in my class.

Each year, previous students would tell the incoming students about the Platinum Club parties and encourage them to strive to be members one day. The concept worked well beyond my imagination. My students always performed at the highest levels regarding benchmarks and annual state assessments.

That popularity among students and parents earned me two "Teacher of the Year" nominations in a row at the school. No matter the setting or student demographics, I strive to think outside the box in the motivation department because I know people need it to perform well. To this day, I run into many past middle school students and marvel at seeing how they've grown into college graduates, career professionals in various fields, and even entrepreneurs. The best part is their shock when they realize I still remember their names- even after all these years.

Transitioning Back to Adult Education

I later got a position at a post-secondary nursing school and then onto a technical college. I teach GED® Social Studies, GED® Reasoning through Language Arts (RLA), and Digital Literacy. I have also had the opportunity to consult teachers at different schools on ways to tweak their classroom structure to engage more with their students.

I witnessed an even greater need for motivation once I transitioned back to teaching adults. Children are required to attend school; however, there is no such mandate with adults. They can stop attending any time, so students' odds of walking away before completion drastically increase.

One Way to Their Mind is Through Their Stomachs

At the first meeting with a new student, I talk with them 1-on-1 to understand why they registered and did not successfully obtain their diplomas in the past. This discussion does not mean a lengthy conversation; it is more so a quick inquiry. I ask them about their obstacles and how I can make them feel more comfortable in class. In addition, I like to know what drives them to be dedicated until the end. I am more concerned with figuring out how to push them instead of just providing them practice in content to pass a test. I want them prepared for college, careers, and life. With their feedback over the years, I discovered that many of them work long hours or even come to school directly from work. They were usually starving when they came to class, so I instituted a coffee table with complimentary coffee, tea, hot chocolate, and a snack such as granola bars, crackers, chips, etc. I even do full meals two to three times per terms, at least one full breakfast and a hot lunch.

Initially, the coffee table was expensive. However, once I had everything stocked, students gladly donated future items to keep it going. I even talked to local businesses for donations, who were happy to give once they heard about a teacher providing refreshments for GED® students. I am always pleasantly surprised at how many of these donors had either gotten their GED® or knew someone who had gotten theirs, so they were happy to support the effort. I often brought in donated baked goods from my church. Students who worked at restaurants gave generously as well. My parents frequently donate food, even when I taught at the middle school. Thanks, Mom and Dad!

Themes Make it Fun

I've been serving food daily at the coffee table for over ten years, and I can't remember ever having the table out of whatever supplies are needed. Students appreciate it immensely and always give back to keep the ball rolling. I would even make food themes for them to look forward to.

Here is a list of some past themes: "Favorite Cereal Day," "DIY PB&J" sandwiches, "Teas from around the World," "It's Cold Outside" (hot cocoa with marshmallows during winter), "Caribbean Patties Day," "Soup-bowl Thursday" (I literally made hot soup), "It's all about the cake," "Use your noodle" (different varieties of ramen noodles), "Rootie-Tootie Fresh and Fruity" (fruits like bananas, oranges, and grapes), "Mango madness" (during the mango season, students would donate mangos from their trees at home to share), "The love of learning" (Valentine's Day goodie bags), "*Donut* forget to study," "Pie-in-your-eye day," "An apple a day" (bowls of various types of apples), and the list goes on.

I solved multiple student issues through this coffee table. One, I fed their natural bodies, so they had the energy for me to feed their minds. Like the candy bar commercial says, "You're not you when you're hungry." Two, it created an atmosphere of family among their classmates, so they gained friends who would encourage one another to reach their goals. Third, the caffeine, sugar rush, or other nourishment helped them wake up and stay more alert during class. That hospitality gained their respect and trust because they knew I cared about them. So, my problem was not getting them to stay, but how do I get them to leave after they passed their exams? It's a good problem to have if you ask me.

You Have to Have a Structure

Every classroom needs structure and routines. Unlike K-12, adult Ed. has the challenge of open enrollment, meaning new students constantly come in throughout the term. Also, students will complete the program at various times. That revolving door means that class structure becomes essential to new students getting acclimated quickly and feeling comfortable about what to do as soon as they walk in. This confidence in what to do immediately alleviates the anxiety they could feel if they come to class late or do not start at the beginning of the semester like everyone else. I created this structure by placing the sign-in sheet on a podium, laying out the materials needed each day on the table near the entryway, displaying all the tasks they will complete on the westside board, and the required times are noted next to each exercise. Also, each table has a basket filled with wipes, hand sanitizer (even before COVID), spare pencils, pens, and highlighters they can borrow.

By setting things up this way, they know to sign in as they enter and immediately turn to the table on their right to collect the documents/ books they need to complete the assignments and quickly determine what stage we are at from the activities and times listed on the board. This routine eliminates them feeling like a deer in headlights when they walk in. If all else fails, they have such a rapport with their colleagues that their comrades will eagerly explain what is happening. That goes back to why the coffee table is essential, and why that sense of community in the classroom is so valuable. It makes life easier for the teacher when students help students.

Let Them Do the Research

Embracing technology in the classroom, particularly for adult students, unlocks a treasure trove of educational benefits. I've seen firsthand how adult learners flourish by integrating tools like PowerPoint and Google Slides into research projects. These projects aren't just about understanding the material; they're about mastering the art of presentation and the skill of digital storytelling. For example, they may have to do a research PowerPoint project on the United States Constitution. As students delve into the historical significance of Constitutional Amendments, they're also honing their tech skills, which are indispensable in today's job market.

The beauty of this approach lies in its dual focus: preparing students for both academic and professional arenas. The class is not merely about acing tests but equipping them with the confidence to navigate complex technology easily. This confidence spills over into their communication abilities, making them more articulate and persuasive.

Moreover, when I pair up the young with the more "seasoned" students, there's a magical interaction. The younger ones often bring a fresh and savvy perspective on technology. At the same time, the older students contribute depth and wisdom to the content. This intergenerational exchange enriches the learning experience, fostering a classroom environment where *everyone is a teacher and a learner.*

As a facilitator, I have the privilege of stepping back and watching my students take charge of their education. The pride they feel upon completing an informative and visually impressive project is evident. It's clear that when adult students are encouraged to use technology, they learn about the past while building the skills they need for the future.

Teach Them to Be Visionaries

I have a saying, "Your high school diploma is not the finish line; it's the starting line." At the beginning of the new year, we do vision boards and focus on determining purpose, manifesting and visualizing goals, and planning for the next steps beyond the diploma. We do this because many students expressed an overwhelming fear of testing and not having a plan once they got their credentials. By addressing students' anxiety and lack of focus, they made progress faster because they were no longer afraid to test, finish, and move on.

Having a vision is like having a compass that guides you through the wilderness of life's challenges and opportunities. Students must have a clear vision to reach their goals because it acts as a beacon of light on the path to success. When students visualize their future, they create a mental blueprint of what they aspire to achieve. Envisioning the end goal helps break down the journey into manageable steps. It's not just about the destination but also the transformation. With a vision, students can align their daily actions with their long-term objectives, ensuring that each step is purposeful and directed toward their ultimate aspirations. This sense of direction and purpose can significantly diminish the fear of the unknown and replace it with confidence and a proactive mindset. Thus, cultivating a solid vision is not just important but essential for students as they navigate through their educational journey and into the broader world.

Connect it to the Real World

Students often ask, "When would I ever use this stuff I'm learning?" Because of this common question, I like incorporating real-world materials for my reading classes, such as sample leasing agreements, contracts, sections from employee handbooks, etc., to show the importance of reading analysis and comprehension. These exercises prove the importance of understanding complex and often lengthy texts. Students need reading stamina to handle reading long documents that are very important to understand. Think about the last time you had to read a long contract, but a quarter of the way through, you got frustrated and just signed on the dotted line to find out later that your signature bound you to something you really didn't like?

By integrating practical documents and real-life scenarios into the curriculum, students begin to see the relevance of their education in their daily lives. For instance, when they dissect a leasing agreement in class, they're not just practicing reading comprehension but preparing to sign their leases confidently. When scrutinizing sections of an employee handbook, they learn to understand workplace expectations and rights. This approach transforms abstract concepts into tangible skills. It bridges the gap between theoretical knowledge and practical application, ensuring that students recognize the value of what they're learning and can apply it when it matters most—in the real, often unpredictable world.

I try to make the history lessons legendary. I don't just *teach* history; I try to bring it to life. When students walk into the classroom, they step into a time machine. They've marched alongside civil rights activists, seen the effects of wars past, debated with the founding fathers, sailed the seven seas with explorers of old, and analyzed the speeches of many presidents and world leaders. As a result of making social studies such an interactive event, most pass the test on the first attempt and often with score beyond passing.

I have spent countless hours scouring for resources that will transport my students through time. My efforts paid off when Carlos, a student who once believed history was just a series of dates to memorize, became so inspired that he decided to attend college to become a teacher. What an honor to plant such a seed and see it harvest in such a manner.

It has been on my wish list for some time to one day bring virtual reality to my classroom. Just imagine If I could take students on virtual field trips around the world or back in time to WW2, I could open their minds to times and places they have never seen before, which would be epic! This tool would be a game-changer for teaching science, too.

Be Their Cheerleader

I am a huge believer in SHOUT OUTS. I make sure to shout out each person via group text and in person whenever a student passes any subject exam. This form of accolade and recognition pushes them to master the next subject until all test parts are completed.

Being a proponent for adult students is a big deal in their educational journey. Adults often juggle numerous responsibilities like work, family, and personal commitments. It's a monumental task requiring much self-discipline and motivation when they decide to hit the books again. That's where the power of positive reinforcement comes in. A shout-out doesn't just acknowledge their effort; it fuels their drive. It's a verbal high-five that says, "I see you, I appreciate you, and I believe in you." This support can light a fire in their bellies to keep going, even when it gets tricky.

Moreover, adult learners sometimes feel isolated in their academic pursuits, especially when studying remotely or in a non-traditional setting. This reason is why creating a community feel is so vital. Celebrating each small victory with a group shout-out fosters a sense of belonging and camaraderie among the students. They don't just see their success; they know the group's collective success, which can be incredibly motivating. It's a reminder that they're not alone in their struggles and that there's a whole team rooting for them. This community spirit helps to build a supportive learning environment where everyone is encouraged to strive for their best.

The impact of recognition on an adult student's confidence cannot be overstated. When you cheer for their accomplishments, you're not just boosting their morale; you're helping them to build a more positive self-image. As they receive praise and recognition for their hard work, they start to internalize this success, which can lead to an increased belief in their abilities. This newfound confidence can spill over into other areas of their lives, making them more willing to take on new challenges and opportunities. It's a Dominoe effect that starts with a simple shout-out but can lead to profound and lasting changes in their personal and professional growth.

Through the strategies I've carefully crafted, I've witnessed remarkable transformations in my students. Their success is a testament to the nurturing environment we've fostered together. They continuously voice their gratitude for the love, support, and confidence I've instilled in them, which fills me with immense pride. I am deeply thankful for the privilege to sow seeds of knowledge and character in their lives, and it's a true honor to observe those seeds flourish into joyous students. That joy extends beyond the classroom, touching the hearts of their families and communities. It's a beautiful cycle of growth and happiness that starts with education and blooms into a legacy of positivity and empowerment.

Chapter 12

They Need Us. Let's Get to Work!

Going back to school, especially after several years, can be challenging and scary, so it is up to the instructors to make their transition back a smooth and reassuring one. Students take a leap of faith to register and hope the path to getting their credential will become clear once they meet their teacher. Day one sets the tone for what may be a smooth or bumpy ride for the student, so the instructor needs to find the time to introduce themself and explain their school's expectations, structure, and testing process. Most students walk through the door with butterflies and anxiety about what to expect, so helping them become comfortable with their new classmates will also be helpful. Even if open enrollment is your school's structure, it will mean having new students enter the class randomly throughout the year. Still, this integral step should never be skipped.

We Are the Knights in Shining Armor

Adult education is a spark of hope, a second chance for learners to reshape their lives and redefine their futures. Many adults return to education to overcome past educational barriers or to adapt to changing job markets. When educators demonstrate a high level of commitment, they validate their students' efforts and reinforce the value of lifelong learning. This commitment can inspire students to persevere despite challenges and strive for excellence. As educators, your example can ignite a passion for learning that transcends the classroom and encourages others within the community to seek personal growth and development.

As adult educators, you are not just teachers, but mentors and guides. You play a vital role in the lives of your students, helping them navigate the complexities of education and life. Students need guidance of all kinds. They need help creating online accounts, discovering how to absorb new knowledge, learning subject content, and scheduling exams. Beyond what they need to study, they need to be reminded *how to study*, and most importantly, students need the boost of confidence that they can do it. Being their cheerleader is a significant part of the job. Having an attitude of "they are all adults" and not taking the time to nurture their morale may prove costly to the student, community, and economy as the teacher observes their class size diminish because students lose hope and choose to quit before receiving their credentials.

By providing top-tier education, you are not just enhancing the lives of individual students, but also contributing to the economic and social well-being of the community at large. Skilled and educated adults are better equipped to participate in the workforce, innovate in their fields, and contribute to their communities' civic and cultural life. Your work is not just about teaching, it's about building a more informed, productive, and cohesive society. You are the architects of a better future.

Don't you think your impact is that big of a deal? Let's imagine a scenario involving an adult student named Alex: Before earning his high school diploma, Alex worked various low-paying jobs, struggling to make ends meet. Education wasn't Alex's priority in his younger years due to his early family responsibilities and a lack of resources. However, recognizing the importance of education later in life, he decided to return to school and earned a high school diploma through an adult education program at a local community school.

With a high school diploma in hand, Alex gained a new sense of confidence and self-worth. This accomplishment provided a solid foundation for lifelong learning and created opportunities for further education through vocational training. Alex's credentials made him eligible for higher-paying jobs that require a minimum of a high school education. His diploma led to a more stable financial situation, allowing him to contribute more to the local economy through spending and taxes.

As a high school graduate, Alex felt more empowered to engage in community activities. He began volunteering at a local food bank, participating in community clean-up events, and attending town hall meetings. This engagement fostered a sense of belonging and responsibility towards the community.

Alex's achievement set a positive example for family members, especially his children and younger relatives. It demonstrated the value of education and resilience, encouraging others to pursue their educational goals. With improved critical thinking and communication skills gained from completing high school, he became more involved in local social issues. Alex joined a community group advocating for better public transportation, which would benefit many who rely on it for work and school.

Education is linked to better health outcomes, so Alex had better access to health information and resources, leading to healthier lifestyle choices. This, in turn, reduced the burden on local health services.

In summary, Alex's journey to obtaining a high school diploma greatly affected his personal growth, employment prospects, community engagement, family inspiration, social advocacy, health and well-being. Each of these areas contributes to a stronger, more resilient community, illustrating how adult education is a personal achievement and a communal asset.

I often ask students if they had attended any other adult ed. programs before coming to my school and why they decided to leave. Unfortunately, some responses include an experience where the teacher rarely spoke to the student directly beyond the first few days. They would express feeling alone even though they were enrolled in a class. They would meet the teacher on day one, who would give them a pretest, after which they would receive a packet to complete at their own pace and turn it in to be graded by the teacher. Later, the teacher would recommend when to take the official test. That's it! While they would have the option to ask a question if they chose, that's the extent of their interactions with the teacher. Some say there was very little to no interaction with their classmates.

In those situations, once the student began taking the test and did not pass, they would become frustrated and stop attending. They would conclude that purchasing a GED® prep book and studying at home would be more convenient since it felt like the experience they encountered in class. Once studying at home proved more complicated than they thought, they would try another GED® test prep location. The detrimental issue with this scenario is that the student probably lost significant time while getting a major blow to their confidence.

Adult learners often bring a wealth of life experiences to the classroom, which, when acknowledged and integrated into the learning process, can enrich the educational experience for all. By valuing and leveraging adult learners' diverse backgrounds and perspectives, educators can create an inclusive and dynamic learning environment that fosters mutual respect and collaboration. This approach enhances the learning experience and prepares students to engage with the diverse world around them with empathy and understanding.

The Greatest Resource is Not a Worksheet

I understand that most adult education centers contain students of all subjects and levels in one classroom. However, limiting student-teacher and student-student interactions to such means is not ideal. Once again, students are more prone to walk away if this is the routine when they go to school. Despite the challenge of having students with such a vast spectrum of functioning levels in one room, there are still interactive ways to assist students in expanding their knowledge of the subject matter.

The best resource for college and career readiness skills content you can give students is opportunities for them to interact with you and their classmates. "Teacher, thanks for this amazing worksheet!" said No Student EVER. They come to class to learn from people, not pages! I am not saying that worksheets or even digital resources are worthless. They are valuable tools that supplement what the instructor brings, but they should be one of many things feeding them. Students should not be given a daily packet to work through alone, nor should they spend each day on digital programs.

If students could pass all their exams simply by reading the information in a book, they would never have registered for classes; they would have only purchased the book and gone at it alone. Remember, we don't want to put total emphasis on passing a test; it should also provide opportunities to hone skills needed for college and careers. I'm referring to communication, collaboration, writing proficiency, critical thinking, analysis, logical reasoning, time management, creativity, active listening, brainstorming, teamwork, adaptability, etc. These skills don't derive from a worksheet.

Adult educators occupy a pivotal position within the educational landscape, one that has the potential to accelerate profound personal and societal transformation. By investing your utmost effort and dedication into teaching, you not only facilitate the acquisition of knowledge and skills but also empower individuals to unlock their full potential. I love mentoring and speaking to other teachers. I aim to remind them of the significance of their role and the far-reaching benefits that stem from their commitment to excellence in education.

We Must be Gentle and Compassionate

How we talk to and treat our students can either build them up or break them down. We must remember that our job includes customer service. I want you to imagine this scenario: Upon entering the boutique, you are immediately drawn to an elegant arrangement of high-end clothing and the soft, ambient music that seems to promise a delightful shopping experience. With a list of items you intend to purchase, you approach a rack of beautifully designed dresses. As you look through the selection, you notice that one of the sales associates is watching you. Still, instead of the expected warm greeting or an offer of assistance, the associate seems disinterested and slightly annoyed.

You attempt to dismiss the initial discomfort and decide to inquire about a particular outfit that caught your eye. As you approach the sales associate, you politely smile and say, "Excuse me, could you please tell me how much this is?"

The response is the opposite of the professionalism and courtesy you anticipated. The associate glances at you and, with an attitude, replies, "It's all on the tag," before turning away to attend to what appears to be a personal text message on their phone.

Taken aback by the dismissive attitude, you feel a growing reluctance to continue shopping. The excitement you felt moments before is replaced by a sense of unwelcomeness. Despite the allure of the items you had hoped to purchase, rewarding such behavior with a sale leaves you disheartened.

With a heavy sigh, you leave the clothes behind and exit the store with the negative encounter lingering in your mind. The experience has not only deterred you from completing your intended purchases but has also instilled a choice to avoid returning to the store in the future. The realization settles in that no matter the quality of the products, the value of respectful and attentive customer service is paramount, and its absence can indeed be a deal-breaker for any potential transaction.

While this book is not about sales, it is about fostering an environment of learning and creating an atmosphere that encourages students to *want* to be in school. Words, tone, and mistreatment can either make or break a student's resolve and lead them to walk away from your school with the intent to never return.

The Effect of Inspirational Teaching

I have had several teachers visit me during my classes and discuss some of the strategies I utilize. They, in turn, explain how their class and curriculum function so that we can strategize how they can take what they witnessed back to their classrooms. I don't believe in being selfish with information. Ideas and inspiration are meant to be shared!

It's all about creating an environment where ideas can flourish and everyone—teachers and students alike—feel empowered to contribute and learn from one another. This open exchange of insights fosters a collaborative atmosphere that can drive innovation in teaching methods and enhance the educational experience for everyone involved.

Sharing knowledge and teaching strategies is like planting seeds that can grow into something more significant than the initial act. Moreover, when teachers are generous with their expertise, they model the collaborative spirit they hope to instill in their students. It shows that education isn't just about what happens in the textbooks but also about how we interact and learn from different perspectives. This approach enriches the academic curriculum to prepare students for the real world, where teamwork and sharing knowledge are invaluable skills. By embedding these values in the classroom, educators are not just teaching; they're shaping the citizens of tomorrow and contributing to a more informed, cooperative society.

The role of an adult educator transcends the boundaries of the classroom, reaching far into the future and across the community. When educators pour their hearts and souls into their vocation, they do not merely impart knowledge; they inspire, motivate, and kindle a lifelong love for learning. The impact of a passionate teacher is immeasurable, often remembered by students long after they have left the school gates.

The Power of High Expectations

Belief in a student's potential is a powerful motivator. When teachers set high expectations, they communicate confidence in their students' abilities, which can drive them to reach new heights. By maintaining a challenging yet supportive learning environment, teachers can foster resilience, encourage perseverance, and help students develop a growth mindset that serves them well beyond their academic years.

While some students enter the class at a lower level, we must keep those students challenged. They must come up, so we shouldn't provide them with "too-easy practice." For instance, if a student scores at an 8th-grade level, we shouldn't give them 8th-grade-level content. We should provide them with practice at a 9th-grade level or higher. When students stop "reaching up," they get bored because the work isn't challenging enough. Another downside of a curriculum that needs to be more rigorous is that it misleads the student into thinking the exam will be as simple as the practice given in class.

Cultivating a Culture of Success

Test scores and academic achievements do not solely define success in the classroom; it also encompasses character development, ethics, and social responsibility. Teachers who give their best create a culture of success that shapes students into well-rounded, empathetic, and engaged citizens. The point is that being a successful student isn't just about getting good grades; it's about becoming a good person. Teachers help with this by teaching students to be ethical, responsible, and kind. Teachers should incorporate strategies for integrating character education into the curriculum and the importance of modeling values such as integrity, respect, and kindness.

Embracing Innovation in Education

The world is changing rapidly, and education must evolve to meet future demands. Teachers who embrace innovation and incorporate technology, project-based learning, and real-world problem-solving into their classrooms prepare their students for the challenges of the 21st century. We must examine current educational trends and offer insights into how teachers can stay at the forefront of pedagogical improvements to ensure their students are equipped with the skills.

In addition, the rapid pace of technological advancements and global changes necessitates an adaptable and continuously evolving workforce. Adult educators are on the front lines of preparing students to meet these demands. By staying informed about the latest trends, tools, and methodologies and integrating these into your teaching, you ensure your students have the most relevant and up-to-date skills.

The Downside of Too Much Screentime

I advocate for digital literacy and technology in the classroom, but I would never suggest that a computer program replace teacher and classmate interactions. Excessive screen time at school can negatively impact students' learning and development. Firstly, it can lead to decreased attention spans and reduced ability to focus on tasks. When students are constantly exposed to screens, whether for educational purposes or not, their brains may become overstimulated, making concentrating on the presented material difficult.

Moreover, excessive screen time can hinder social interaction and communication skills. Classroom environments should foster peer-to-peer interactions and teacher-student engagement, which are essential for developing social skills and collaborative learning. Over-reliance on screens may limit these opportunities for face-to-face interaction and hinder the development of interpersonal skills.

Too much screen time can also contribute to physical health issues such as eyestrain, headaches, and poor posture. Extended periods of staring at screens can strain the eyes and lead to discomfort, detracting from students' ability to engage with classroom activities effectively.

Furthermore, excessive screen time can potentially exacerbate inequalities among students. Not all students may have equal access to technology or be comfortable using it extensively, so relying too heavily on screens for instruction may disadvantage students who are less proficient with technology or who do not have access to it outside of the classroom.

Overall, while technology can be a valuable tool for enhancing learning experiences, educators need to balance and incorporate various teaching methods to support students' holistic development, including face-to-face interactions, hands-on activities, and other non-screen-based approaches.

The Lifelong Impact of Mentorship

Mentorship is one of the most valuable gifts a teacher can offer. Educators can guide students through personal and academic challenges, providing support that often exists by taking on the role of mentors in their professional lives. This section highlights the lasting benefits of mentorship, including increased academic success, higher self-esteem, and improved social skills. It also provides practical advice for teachers on becoming influential mentors and building meaningful connections with their students.

As a mentor for students, I have individuals I taught years ago who continue to seek my advice and guidance. That reminds me of the powerful trust I've gained from them, so I don't take it lightly. I use the *Remind* app to keep communication open with students. However, once they finish my class, they still have this medium of contact to reach me, even years later, to ask questions or to check in on how I'm doing. I often get a random message from a past student letting me know how far they have reached in their journey. I get constant notifications about their post-secondary graduations, new jobs, family events like baby announcements, weddings, and holiday greetings.

Mentorship in education transcends the traditional teacher-student dynamic, creating a profound bond. When educators become mentors, they become confidants, coaches, and cheerleaders, offering guidance beyond textbooks and test scores. This relationship allows students to see their mentors as role models whose wisdom and experience are invaluable in navigating the complexities of life. By providing a safe space for open communication, mentors help students tackle academic hurdles and personal challenges that can impede success in and out of the classroom. These mentored students are often better prepared to face the future, knowing they have a supportive guide to help them manage life's twists and turns.

For educators looking to embrace the mantle of mentorship, the journey involves much more than a willingness to help. It requires active listening, patience, and a genuine interest in the individual growth of their mentees. Influential mentors recognize each student's strengths and weaknesses, tailoring their support to meet those needs. They celebrate successes, provide constructive feedback, and, most importantly, instill a sense of possibility and ambition in their students. By sharing their experiences and showing vulnerability, mentors can strengthen the trust and respect in the relationship, making their advice more impactful.

I hope these words underscore the transformative power of mentorship and guide educators in cultivating these critical relationships. This strategy to connect with students on a deeper level, fosters an environment where mentorship can thrive, and students can emerge as empowered, self-assured individuals ready to contribute positively to society.

Section 3

To the Higher-Ups

(Legislatures and Administrators)

Chapter 13

Understanding the Importance of Career Pathways in Education

For school administrators and policymakers, this book provides suggestions for fostering an educational environment that helps adult learners flourish. These leaders can shape educational policies and create programs that can accommodate the unique needs of adult students. The strategies discussed in the book are meant to inspire innovative thinking and action.

Urgent Action Needed: Instilling Career Readiness in Middle School, High School, and Beyond

Allow me to rewind and look back before we move forward. Yes, this is still about adults, but it is best to target the middle and high school levels *before* they reach age 16, when they become eligible to become adult education students. I have asked numerous underage students about their career goals to find out they have yet to decide what field they want to pursue. They are not eager to go anywhere since they don't know which way to go. In today's rapidly evolving world, preparing students for their future careers is more crucial than ever before. Gone are the days when a one-size-fits-all education model sufficed. To meet students' diverse needs and aspirations, schools must embrace career and technical education (CTE) pathways that offer specialized training in fields such as health science, business, distribution and logistics, information technology, hospitality, manufacturing, etc. By doing so, schools can equip students with the skills and knowledge necessary to thrive in the workforce sooner.

Companies are now so eager for qualified, skilled employees that they are taking the reins and creating in-house training programs to get people trained and ready to work faster to meet their needs. The problem companies face is that there are more job opportunities than skilled workers to fill the positions. The last thing schools would want is for companies to step on their toes and compete with the traditional education system. This tension between the rapidly evolving demands of the job market and the more conventional approaches to education has sparked debates about the effectiveness of current educational models in preparing students for the workforce. While schools strive to impart a broad range of knowledge and critical thinking skills, many argue that they often fail to provide the specific, job-ready skills that employers seek. This gap has led to calls for greater collaboration between educational institutions and industries to ensure curricula align with the workforce's needs, ultimately benefiting both students and employers.

Back when I was in middle school, we had classes like wood shop, home economics, typing, and life skills, which taught us how to manage money and pay bills. We also learned cursive, library research, Roman numerals, and driver's ed (*the good old days*). Unfortunately, many schools have removed such courses because of the mandates on high-stakes testing. As a result, students today often graduate without the essential practical skills that were once considered integral to a well-rounded education. The emphasis on standardized testing has narrowed the curriculum, prioritizing subjects like math, science, and language arts at the expense of hands-on learning and life skills. This shift has left many young adults entering the workforce, higher education, and adulthood lacking essential competencies such as financial literacy, basic home maintenance, and necessary soft skills.

Building a Foundation: Implementing CTE Programs

Middle school serves as a critical juncture in a student's educational journey. It's a time when young minds explore their interests and passions, laying the groundwork for future academic and career pursuits. School districts should seize this opportunity to introduce students to various career pathways through engaging and interactive courses *starting at the middle school level*. Do not wait. Imagine, if a student discovered a love of carpentry, began studying it at their middle school, and continued honing those skills throughout high school. They could graduate with YEARS of employable experience! Even if the student had to transition to adult education later on, they would already be on a career pathway with foundational knowledge for a job. A company would eagerly hire that individual when they graduate high school or obtain their GED®.

School districts should take that perfect window of opportunity to show students a variety of different career options with fun and interactive classes, such as:

Exploratory Courses: Middle schools should not delay offering exploratory courses that expose students to various career fields. These courses could include introductory modules in health science, business fundamentals, basic technology skills, culinary arts, environmental science, media production, and introductory engineering. Early exposure to these fields can help students make informed decisions about their future careers, and it's a crucial step that we need to take NOW.

Hands-on Learning: Incorporating hands-on learning experiences is essential in middle school CTE programs. Whether through interactive labs, field trips to local businesses, or guest speakers from industry professionals, students should have opportunities to apply their knowledge in real-world settings. When I think back to when I was in school, the things I learned in home economics helped me once I became an adult and mom. Who doesn't need to learn skills such as cooking, sewing basics, and simple ways to keep areas clean?

Career Counseling: Middle school is an ideal time to begin career exploration and counseling, which should continue through the adult education level. School counselors and educators should collaborate to help students identify their interests, strengths, and career goals and guide them toward appropriate CTE pathways.

As students transition from middle school to high school, they should have access to more specialized CTE courses tailored to their interests and career aspirations. High school CTE programs should provide in-depth training and hands-on experiences that prepare students for success in their chosen fields.

Structured Pathways: High schools should offer structured CTE pathways aligned with industry standards and workforce demands. These pathways may include advanced courses in health sciences, business management, IT and computer science, culinary arts, and advanced manufacturing.

Work-Based Learning: To bridge the gap between classroom learning and real-world application, high school CTE programs should incorporate work-based learning opportunities such as internships, apprenticeships, and cooperative education programs. These experiences allow students to gain valuable skills, network with professionals, and explore potential career paths firsthand.

Industry Certifications: High school CTE programs should emphasize attaining industry-recognized certifications and credentials. These certifications validate students' skills and competencies and enhance their employability and readiness for post-secondary education or workforce entry.

Ensuring Equity and Access for All Students

In implementing CTE programs, school districts must prioritize equity and access to ensure that all students, regardless of background or socioeconomic status, can participate and succeed. Here are some elements to consider:

Inclusive Recruitment: Schools should actively recruit students from diverse backgrounds and underserved communities into CTE programs. Outreach efforts should target students who may not traditionally consider careers in these fields, including students of color, low-income students, and students with disabilities.

Removing Barriers: School districts should identify and address barriers that may hinder students' participation in CTE programs, such as transportation limitations, financial constraints, or academic prerequisites. By providing adequate support services and resources, schools can ensure that all students have an equal opportunity to pursue their career interests.

Culturally Relevant Curriculum: The CTE curriculum should be culturally relevant and responsive to the needs and interests of all students. Schools should incorporate diverse perspectives, examples, and case studies into their course materials, ensuring that students see themselves reflected in the content and feel valued and included in the learning process.

Collaborating with Stakeholders for Success

The success of CTE programs relies on collaboration and partnership among various stakeholders, including educators, employers, industry professionals, parents, and community organizations. Here are some things to think about:

Industry Partnerships: Schools should collaborate with local businesses, industries, and professional organizations to develop curricula, provide guest speakers, offer work-based learning opportunities, and secure internships or apprenticeships for students. These partnerships help align CTE programs with industry needs and ensure students receive relevant and up-to-date training.

Parent and Community Engagement: Schools should actively involve parents and community members in supporting CTE programs. This engagement may include hosting informational sessions, parent workshops, career fairs, or industry showcases to demonstrate the benefits of CTE education and garner community support.

Professional Development: Educators involved in CTE programs should receive ongoing professional development and training to stay abreast of industry trends, teaching methodologies, and technological advancements. Investing in teachers' professional growth ensures that CTE programs remain rigorous, relevant, and impactful for students.

Data proves that integrating such practices can increase student engagement toward lucrative employment while boosting the incentive to complete their education. For example, according to an article in U.S. News and World Report, "States use a variety of federal, state and local funds to pay for CTE programs, and the arguments for bigger investments in CTE programming are supported by research. 'High school students who complete at least two course credits in a career pathway have about a 95% graduation rate,' according to federal data – roughly 10% higher than the national average." As we reflect on the evolution of education, there's a growing recognition of the need to reintegrate practical, real-world learning experiences into the curriculum to better prepare students for the challenges they'll face beyond the classroom.

By integrating career and technical education (CTE) pathways that begin in middle and high schools and extend into adult education, school districts can empower students to explore their interests, develop essential skills, and prepare for successful careers in today's competitive global economy. This approach aims to keep students engaged in traditional high school settings, reducing dropout rates, as they would have a clearer understanding of their goals and potential career paths. Moreover, if promising job opportunities awaited them upon graduation, students would be more motivated to stay in school. Through hands-on learning, internships, collaborations with industries, and ensuring equal opportunities, schools can ensure that all students graduate equipped with the knowledge, skills, and confidence needed to pursue their aspirations and make meaningful contributions to society.

Chapter 14

We Got Child Support, but what about Adult Support?

The idea that education concludes with a graduation ceremony is a common misconception. In reality, education is a never-ending path that continues to unfold throughout our lives. This concept is central to the book, which serves as a reminder that learning does not stop when one receives a diploma. Instead, it is a lifelong journey that evolves with our experiences and challenges. The book is designed to speak to those who recognize the value of continuous learning and those who support adult learners in their pursuit of knowledge and skills. It underscores the notion that education is not just for the young but for anyone at any age who desires to grow intellectually and professionally.

Basically, this could involve giving adults more options for learning, like classes in the evenings or online. They might also offer courses that help with practical life skills. The idea is to make it easier for adults to fit learning into their busy lives, like juggling work and family responsibilities.

Unlocking Potential: Empowering Adult Learners in School Districts

Various services and forms of support can enhance the educational experience for adults. The report recognizes that adult learners often face different challenges than traditional students, including tighter schedules, financial responsibilities, and the need to juggle personal commitments.

It suggests that educational institutions should offer tailored services such as career counseling, financial aid advice, and study support groups specifically designed for adult students. These services are intended to help adult learners navigate the complexities of returning to school and to support them in achieving their educational goals.

I also emphasize the importance of community and peer support in the success of adult learners. Going back to school after a hiatus can be intimidating, and a community that understands and supports the unique journey of adult learners can be incredibly beneficial. Educational institutions can significantly improve adult learners' chances of success by fostering a sense of belonging and providing a network for sharing experiences and resources. The strategies outlined in the book aim to build these supportive communities and ensure that adult learners are welcomed and celebrated as they continue their lifelong educational journey.

Digital Literacy – The Key to the Modern World & Bridging the Digital Divide

Digital proficiency has become as fundamental as reading and writing in the modern world. We can never forget the days of the COVID pandemic; however, this unprecedented era has made the integration of technology a part of almost every aspect of daily life, from banking to healthcare to transportation to shopping and everything in between, so the ability to navigate the digital landscape is crucial. As centers of education and learning, school districts are uniquely positioned to bridge the digital divide by providing digital literacy courses designed for adult learners. Doing so ensures that all community members can acquire essential skills that are increasingly required for employment, personal management, and informed citizenship.

Offering courses focusing on basic computer skills is foundational in fostering digital literacy. These skills include understanding how to operate a computer or a smartphone, using word processors, and managing files and folders. These are not intuitive tasks for many adults who did not grow up with technology. Remember, the GED® test is computer-based, so imagine the frustrations of students who struggle to type their extended response essays or fumble to complete drag-and-drop questions. Don't get me started on the panic some encounter when their computer screen does something out of the ordinary. Courses can demystify computers and empower individuals to engage with technology confidently. This empowerment can improve job prospects, as computer proficiency is a prerequisite for many positions in today's workforce.

I have had many students ask for my assistance to do things most of us take for granted. For example, I have had to help many students send a text message or download an app on *their* cell phone (some didn't even know which button was for composing messages), navigate a website to complete an online application, send an email with an attachment, or typing up a resume. Many of these students made it known that when they asked a younger family member for assistance, it was often met with great annoyance, or the person failed to show them how to do it but instead did it for them out of a lack of patience. Hence, they never learned to do it for themselves.

My dear friend recounted a troubling situation when her mother urgently needed transportation while she was in an unfamiliar area. Since her mother lives in another state, my friend attempted to guide her through downloading the Uber app over the phone to arrange a ride home. However, her mother struggled to navigate her phone to find and download the app, and even after managing to do so, she couldn't figure out how to use it to request a ride. Consequently, she had to walk a considerable distance to find a stranger who could assist her. It was a difficult situation for my friend, but even more so for her mother, who had to put herself at risk to reach safety.

Internet safety is another critical component of digital literacy. As more personal information and sensitive data are shared online, knowing how to protect oneself from cyber threats cannot be overstated. School districts providing internet safety courses would equip adult learners with the knowledge to recognize scams, create strong passwords, and maintain privacy online. This education is beneficial not only for individuals but also for the broader community as it helps create a safer digital environment for everyone.

Navigating online learning platforms has become necessary for lifelong learning. The internet is a treasure trove of educational resources, from online courses to instructional videos and academic articles. However, the sheer volume of information can be overwhelming, and not all are credible or valuable. By teaching adults how to find and use reputable online learning platforms, school districts can open doors to continuous education. This skill promotes a culture of learning and adaptation, which is vital for personal growth and staying relevant in an ever-evolving job market.

Incorporating such a curriculum should be a standard component, not something that is seen as an elective. School districts are critical in ensuring that adult learners are included in the digital age. By offering comprehensive digital literacy courses covering basic computer skills, internet safety, and online learning platforms, they can provide the tools for adults to thrive in a technology-driven society. This investment in adult education is an investment in the community's future, fostering an environment where everyone can succeed and contribute meaningfully to our digital world.

While there are tons of resources available to school districts, here are a few resources:

- *DigitalLearn.org* provides comprehensive computer and technology training covering hardware, software, applications, and essential job search resources. The platform offers facilitator support for course utilization and customization, catering to self-guided and self-paced community learners, particularly beneficial for visual learners with lower literacy levels. (Lessons are available in English and Spanish)
- Techboomers.com is an educational website helping older adults and novice users learn fundamental computer skills and navigate the digital world. It provides articles and tutorials on using computers, social media, applications, and online platforms. Lessons cover various topics, guiding users using devices, applications, and more. The resource is beneficial for enhancing digital literacy. (Lessons are available in English)
- *GCFLearnFree.org* offers a website with free resources and tools for learners to acquire essential 21st-century skills such as Microsoft Office, email, reading, and math. With over 180 topics, 2,000 lessons, 800+ videos, and 55+ interactives and games, it caters to self-guided learners needing more in-depth training and guidance for their digital literacy journey. Basic literacy skills are required for utilization. (Lessons are available in English and Spanish)

- *The Mozilla Foundation* provides free and open-source tools and resources for facilitators to conduct sessions on web literacy, covering topics like basic web literacy, coding, and data protection. The materials offer guidance on facilitation and community engagement, making it ideal for facilitators aiming to enhance their in-person or virtual group sessions. (Curriculum and Courses are available in English)
- *Google for Education*, Applied Digital Skills provides a comprehensive curriculum encompassing over 1,000 topics for teachers. The platform allows integration into Google Classrooms or direct teaching through the program. It offers a course on teaching with the platform and options for self-guided learners to access and follow classes independently. (Courses are offered in English)

In my adult digital literacy class, I utilize the Google for Education platform, which offers numerous free curriculums and teacher certification training for schools and educators. Additionally, at my technical college, I incorporate Grow with Google's free online curriculum to facilitate hands-on learning experiences in areas such as word processing, spreadsheets, keyboarding, design, and more.

Consider this scenario: John, a 45-year-old retail manager, felt left behind in the digital world. He had all the expertise in the retail field but lacked the knowledge to perform tasks that utilized technology. Out of fear that his job could be at risk to a younger, more tech-savvy associate, he enrolled in a digital literacy course offered by his local school district. Within a few months, John confidently used a computer for work and learning, which opened new career opportunities.

Financial Assistance – Investing in Success

One of the most critical impediments to adult education is the financial barrier. To support adult learners, school districts can implement various financial assistance options. These may include scholarships, sliding-scale tuition fees based on income levels, and establishing partnerships with local businesses for sponsorships and tuition reimbursement programs. By offering such support, educational opportunities become more financially available to adult learners, helping them overcome this significant obstacle to furthering their education.

In addition to scholarships and sliding-scale tuition fees, providing income-based bus passes can help adult students manage transportation costs, ensure regular class attendance, and aid in pursuing their academic goals. Many students resort to costly ride-hailing services like Lyft and Uber, leading to financial strains that may deter consistent attendance and eventually result in dropping out of classes.

Educational institutions can enhance financial support for adult learners by offering book vouchers to help alleviate the costs of essential textbooks and learning materials. Including book vouchers in their support mechanisms can significantly reduce the financial burden of pursuing education, ultimately creating a more accessible learning environment for adult students.

The story of Sara, a single mother of two, exemplifies the transformation possible with adequate financial assistance. Despite the challenges of juggling work and family responsibilities, Sara harbored the dream of getting her diploma. Through the financial assistance program provided by her school district, Sara managed tuition costs while maintaining her job and caring for her family. This essential support enabled Sara to achieve her goal of getting her credential and opened doors to a better-paying job, significantly improving her and her children's prospects. Sara's success story underscores the profound impact that targeted financial assistance can have on individuals striving to better themselves and their circumstances.

Incentives for Completion – Motivation to Succeed

Incentives play a vital role in driving adult learners towards program completion. School districts can introduce various motivating factors within educational settings to encourage students to finish their programs successfully. These incentives may include recognizing milestones, such as providing certificates upon course completion or offering tangible rewards like book vouchers or discounts on future courses for individuals who complete a program. School districts can effectively inspire and support adult learners on their educational journeys by incorporating such incentives, fostering a culture of achievement and continuous learning.

Celebrating milestones to motivate adult students to obtain their high school diploma, several incentive ideas can be employed:

Career Pathways: Emphasize the diverse career opportunities that open up with a GED. Highlight success stories of GED graduates who have progressed in their careers, showcasing real-world examples of the doors that can open through education.

Small Rewards: Consider implementing a system of small rewards, such as gift cards, to recognize and incentivize students as they reach specific milestones during GED preparation. My school provides a pin that displays the subject a student has successfully passed toward their diploma. These rewards can serve as tangible acknowledgments of progress, offering encouragement and reinforcing the value of effort and commitment in the educational journey.

Let's use this example scenario about David's journey and how it would exemplify the power of incentivizing program completion: David embarked on a GED program but faced challenges in maintaining motivation. However, by implementing a completion incentive program that would give him a discount on a tech program offered within his school district, David discovered the additional drive he required to persevere. This newfound motivation propelled him to complete his certification successfully. As a result of his dedication and hard work, David received a voucher as a reward. This voucher played a pivotal role in assisting him in acquiring the necessary tools for pursuing his new trade, underscoring how tailored incentives can inspire individuals to achieve their educational goals and empower them to transition into new opportunities with the necessary resources and support.

Flexible Learning Options – Fitting School into Life

Adult learners juggle so much in their lives - work, family duties, personal commitments - all while pursuing their education. Online courses have emerged as a cornerstone of flexible education, allowing adult learners to study at their own pace and convenience. By accessing course materials remotely, individuals can harmonize their learning with existing familial, professional, or personal commitments. They give adult learners the power to control their learning pace and location. From late-night study sessions to early morning assignments, online courses mold seamlessly to fit into any schedule. Plus, the interactive tools and resources? They turn learning into a dynamic experience, making education a rewarding journey rather than a daunting task.

This option works best in a synchronous platform where students work independently. Still, an asynchronous format provides more outstanding guidance in students' learning when they periodically meet with their instructors live online. It's like dancing through a busy day with a dozen tasks, each one vital. But guess what? Educational institutions get it. They see these challenges and step up to make things easier for adult learners by offering a buffet of flexible learning options. It's like saying, "We've got your back!"

Picture this: evening classes, the saving grace for those hustling during the day. These classes offer a lifeline, letting individuals catch lessons and dive into coursework after their workday. And then, there are weekend workshops, like intense learning opportunities tailor-made for folks with jam-packed weekdays. It's a chance to focus entirely on learning when the world around them slows down a bit.

By offering these flexible options, educational institutions aren't just meeting adult learners halfway; they're holding out a helping hand, saying, "We see you, we get you, and we're here to make this journey smoother." It's about breaking barriers and making education a welcoming place for all, regardless of the chaos life throws their way. Through such tailored support, adult learners can easily navigate their academic pursuits and achieve their educational aspirations.

Support Systems – Building a Community of Learners

When it comes to adult education, creating a truly supportive environment is vital to succeeding and staying motivated and engaged as they navigate their educational journeys. It's like having a guiding light in a maze of learning possibilities. Mentorship programs are like having a personal cheerleader cheering them on, offering guidance tailored precisely to what adult learners need. They help adult students tackle challenges head-on, set crucial learning goals, and provide that extra push when they need it most, all while making them feel like they truly belong in this educational community.

Imagine being part of a study group within your school district—like being on a learning adventure with friends. These groups help them better understand complex course materials and boost their confidence by sharing insights and working together on assignments. Through this collaborative process, they don't just learn; they forge connections with peers who inspire and motivate them, creating a supportive environment where they lift each other and celebrate their achievements.

And let's remember to empower networking events. Picture them mingling with professionals and fellow learners, gaining valuable insights into their field of interest, and exploring career paths they might have yet to consider. These events are like gateways to new opportunities, enriching their educational experiences and empowering them to build relationships that can shape their academic and professional futures. So, by fostering a strong sense of community through mentorship, study groups, and networking gatherings, their school districts aren't just nurturing their growth—they're paving the way for their success in every step of their educational journey.

A Brighter Future for All

Supporting adult learners is an investment in the individual and the community. By implementing innovative services like digital literacy courses, financial assistance, and flexible learning options, school districts can help adult learners unlock their potential and achieve their dreams. Let's work together to make lifelong learning accessible and rewarding for everyone.

Remember, the journey of education never truly ends; it evolves with us, offering new beginnings and brighter futures.

Chapter 15

Give Honor Where Honor is Due

All educators matter; however, the contributions of *adult* educators often go underappreciated. School administrators and policymakers hold the key to recognizing and honoring these vital individuals who play a crucial role in shaping the educational journeys of adult learners. When you look at many of the rewards and awards given to teachers, most target K-12 educators. Many organizations and school districts overlook the significant role adult educators play in society. By acknowledging and supporting adult educators, these entities can foster a culture of respect, professionalism, and growth within the academic community, making each member feel valued and integral to its success.

Understanding the Role of Adult Educators

Adult educators face unique challenges in the educational landscape, such as dealing with diverse student backgrounds, assisting students across a wide spectrum of ages, managing students' complex life situations that affect learning, and addressing the specific needs of adult learners. They bring a wealth of experience, expertise, and dedication, guiding adult learners to personal and professional development. Recognizing the importance of their role is the first step in honoring their contributions and addressing these specific challenges they face.

Communities benefit greatly from the efforts of adult educators. By providing accessible and high-quality training opportunities, adult educators empower individuals to enhance their skills, knowledge, and abilities. This, in turn, leads to increased employability, higher income potential, and improved quality of life for community members. When adults are equipped with the tools they need to succeed, they become active contributors to the local economy and society, fostering economic growth and social cohesion. While educating children is a noble act that directly influences the child, educating adults is a powerful endeavor that not only transforms households and neighborhoods but also positively impacts the children within those communities.

Moreover, adult educators often serve as catalysts for community change and development. They address adults' specific needs and challenges in their community, whether improving literacy rates, supporting workforce development, or promoting lifelong learning. By collaborating with local organizations, employers, and other stakeholders, adult educators create partnerships that enhance community and economic development initiatives. Their work helps bridge the gap between the education system and the demands of the local job market, ensuring that individuals have the skills and qualifications needed to thrive.

The efforts of adult educators have far-reaching benefits for communities. From enhancing individuals' employability and income potential to driving economic growth and fostering community development, adult educators play a vital role in shaping the future of their communities. Recognizing and celebrating their achievements not only honors their dedication but also serves as a powerful testament to the transformative power of education, inspiring us all to continue our work in this field.

Recognizing Achievement and Excellence

Much like those in place for K-12, creating mechanisms to recognize and celebrate the achievements of adult educators is essential. This could include establishing awards for innovation in teaching, commendations for outstanding student outcomes, and acknowledgment programs for educators who have made significant contributions to the field. These initiatives can motivate those educators, boost morale, and highlight their valuable impact on adult learners. While such events exist at state or national levels by organizations such as the Coalition on Adult Basic

Education (COABE) and Career, Technical, Adult & Community Education (CTACE), these celebrations should also occur at the local levels.

One way to emphasize the importance of adult educators is by establishing annual or biannual adult-educator awards ceremonies dedicated explicitly to honoring their achievements. These events would serve as a platform to publicly celebrate and commend outstanding educators for their dedication, innovation, and impact on adult learners. By inviting teachers, community members, and stakeholders to attend and participate, the ceremony can create a positive and supportive atmosphere that uplifts the entire profession and underscores the significance of their contributions.

In addition to awards ceremonies, creating a system of ongoing recognition can also be highly effective. This process can be done through monthly or quarterly publications where educators are nominated by their students for their exceptional work. The commendations can be publicly announced and showcased in staff rooms or online platforms, such as the district or organization's website or social media pages.

Incorporating the voices of adult learners in the recognition process can also be powerful. Establishing student-led awards allows learners to express gratitude and appreciation for the educators who have significantly impacted their lives. This not only honors the educators but also fosters a sense of community and shared responsibility for learning. By involving and empowering adult learners in the recognition process, institutions emphasize the collaborative nature of education and create a space for positive feedback and dialogue, enhancing the overall learning environment.

Furthermore, leveraging technology and social media platforms can expand the reach and impact of recognition programs. Creating online communities or forums where educators can share their achievements, experiences, and best practices promotes collaboration and provides a platform for others to learn from and be inspired by their peers.

There are several impactful ways to recognize and celebrate the achievements of adult educators. Organizations can cultivate a positive and supportive environment that celebrates excellence and encourages continuous growth through awards ceremonies, ongoing commendation programs, professional development opportunities, student-led recognition, and leveraging technology. By implementing these strategies, we can uplift adult educators, showcase their invaluable contributions, and ultimately enhance the quality and impact of adult education.

School administrators and policymakers should actively celebrate the contributions and achievements of adult educators, fostering a culture of gratitude, recognition, and respect within the educational community.

Supporting Well-being and Work-Life Balance

I mentioned in a previous chapter that adult educators become privy to challenging circumstances in their students' lives, so prioritizing adult educators' well-being and work-life balance is crucial. Policies promoting self-care, mental health support, and flexible working arrangements can prevent burnout and ensure a healthy and motivated staff. One idea to support the well-being of adult educators is to provide them with regular opportunities for self-care. This approach can include wellness programs, such as yoga or meditation classes, mindfulness training, or access to a local gym or exercise facility. This perk could be offered through the district's insurance provider or in partnership with vendors in this area. By encouraging educators to care for their physical and mental health, they are better equipped to manage stress and maintain a positive mindset. Additionally, providing mental health support, such as access to counseling or therapy services, can be invaluable for educators dealing with personal or professional challenges.

Another idea is offering professional development opportunities that include workshops or seminars on time management, stress reduction techniques, or strategies for maintaining a healthy work-life balance. Additionally, mentoring or coaching programs can provide educators with the guidance and support they need to navigate their professional challenges and effectively manage their responsibilities.

I cannot begin to express the many encounters I've had with students who have shared heart-wrenching circumstances that I was unable to assist with, but desperately wished I could have done something to minimize the students' suffering. One such example was a student whose toddler-aged son was murdered by her boyfriend while she was at work. I referred her to the school's counselor, but as a mom, my heart broke as she shared her story and how she promised her son that she would get her diploma just before his passing. In addition to the countless students who bring with them issues stemming from their past traumatic experiences in the criminal justice system, homelessness, abuse and long-term unemployment. When the students hurt, so do their teachers. By equipping educators with self-care skills and support systems, they are better prepared to handle the demands of their profession while still taking care of themselves.

Overall, supporting adult educators' well-being and work-life balance is essential for creating a positive and thriving teaching environment. By implementing policies and programs prioritizing self-care, mental health, and flexible working arrangements, educators are better equipped to bring their best selves to their work and ultimately provide a high-quality educational experience to their students.

Providing Resources and Tools

Equipping adult educators with the necessary resources, technology, and tools is pivotal in enabling them to deliver high-quality education. Policymakers should allocate adequate resources to support educators' teaching endeavors, ensuring smooth and effective instructional delivery.

Access to modern technology and tools can enhance the teaching experience and make learning more engaging and interactive for adult students. These technological advancements, from interactive whiteboards and multimedia presentations to online platforms and virtual learning environments, can open new avenues for adult educators to connect with their students and create dynamic learning experiences.

Advocating for Recognition and Advancement

School administrators and policymakers can advocate for the recognition and advancement of adult educators within the educational system. This plan can involve lobbying for fair compensation, career advancement opportunities, and inclusion in decision-making processes. Advocating for fair compensation is crucial to attracting and retaining high-quality adult educators. Many adult educators work on a part-time basis, which may limit their access to benefits and stable income. By advocating for fair wages and benefits, school leaders can demonstrate their commitment to valuing the work of adult educators and creating sustainable career paths for them.

Offering career advancement opportunities for adult educators is another way to recognize and support their contributions by providing professional growth pathways, mentorship programs, leadership roles, and opportunities to pursue advanced degrees or certifications. Investing in the professional development of adult educators, administrators, and policymakers enhances their skills and knowledge and demonstrates a commitment to their long-term success and fulfillment within the field.

Including adult educators in decision-making ensures their expertise and perspectives are represented. Administrators and policymakers can establish advisory committees or task forces comprised of adult educators to provide input on curriculum development, program design, and policy implementation. By actively involving adult educators in these processes, administrators, and policymakers can tap into their valuable insights and expertise, ultimately leading to more effective and learner-centered adult education programs.

Furthermore, administrators and policymakers can collaborate with adult educators to advocate for policy changes that address adult learners' unique needs and challenges. These teachers are on the front lines and have firsthand experience of adult learners' barriers, such as limited access to affordable childcare, transportation, or support services. Administrators and policymakers can identify and address these systemic challenges by working together, making adult education more accessible and equitable.

Embracing Diversity and Inclusion

Promoting diversity and inclusivity within adult education is essential. Staff should be as diverse as the student populations they teach. School administrators and policymakers should actively create a welcoming and inclusive environment that celebrates the diversity of adult educators and learners.

Including diverse perspectives and experiences in decision-making processes can lead to more innovative and practical solutions to the challenges faced in adult education. Administrators and policymakers can encourage diversity by actively seeking out and recruiting adult educators from underrepresented groups, providing training and support for cultural competence and inclusion, and fostering a supportive and inclusive workplace culture to help create an environment where all adult educators feel valued, respected, and empowered to contribute their unique insights and perspectives.

Another important aspect of promoting diversity and inclusivity is ensuring that adult education programs are culturally responsive and address diverse adult learners' specific needs and goals. Administrators and policymakers can work with adult educators to develop culturally relevant curricula, establish support services that cater to learners' diverse needs, and provide professional development opportunities for adult educators to enhance their cultural competency and understanding.

Here are five positive and actionable tips for promoting diversity and inclusivity in adult education:

1. Embrace diversity in staff: Ensure a diverse teaching staff that reflects the student population they serve will create a welcoming environment for all learners.
2. Provide training on diversity and inclusion: Offer professional development opportunities to educators that focus on cultural competence and inclusive teaching practices.
3. Incorporate diverse perspectives in decision-making: Seek input from educators with diverse backgrounds and experiences to ensure a more inclusive decision-making process.
4. Foster a supportive and inclusive culture: Create a work environment that celebrates diversity, respects all individuals, and promotes collaboration and mutual understanding.
5. Teach with respect for all learners: Develop and implement teaching approaches that acknowledge and respond to adult students' unique needs, experiences, and backgrounds.

By following these positive steps, adult education programs can create an inclusive and empowering learning environment for all learners and educators.

Engaging in Continuous Feedback and Evaluation

Regular feedback and evaluation mechanisms should be in place to assess adult educators' needs, challenges, and successes. School administrators and policymakers can use this feedback to make informed decisions, implement improvements, and provide tailored support.

For example, let's consider a common scenario in an adult education setting: a diverse group of adult learners enrolled in an English as a Second Language (ESL) program. To promote diversity and inclusivity in this scenario, the program could ensure that the teaching staff reflects the students' cultural and linguistic backgrounds. This strategy creates a welcoming and relatable environment where learners can see themselves represented and feel more comfortable expressing their unique perspectives and experiences.

Regular feedback from both learners and educators would be valuable in this scenario. Feedback from learners could provide insights into their individual learning preferences, cultural considerations, and any potential barriers they may be facing. Educators can use this feedback to tailor their teaching approaches and materials accordingly. Additionally, educators can provide feedback on their experiences teaching a diverse group, sharing any challenges they may face and suggesting ongoing training and support to enhance their effectiveness in promoting diversity and inclusivity.

The transformative power of adult education lies not only in the knowledge and skills imparted but also in the created inclusive and empowering learning environment. School leaders can take adult education to new heights by recognizing and honoring the valuable contributions of adult educators, promoting diversity and inclusivity, and engaging in continuous feedback and evaluation. By valuing and supporting these instructors, we can unlock their full potential and create a brighter future for students, communities, and society. It is time to amaze ourselves and take the necessary steps to ensure adult education reaches new heights of excellence and impact.

Special Thanks

To my students over the years who have honored me the ability to be a part of your lives, trusted me to guide you along the way and encouraged me to write this book to help people I may never get to meet to be encouraged in their desire to go back to school. Thanks Keri, my good friend and old college classmate, for having my back by encouraging me to get this book published and spreading the word to others about the power contained within its pages and always taking the time to bounce ideas around. Thanks, Mom and Dad, for always being the first to jump on board to support whatever I put my hands to while quickly telling the world how proud of me you are. I want to shout out my kids for their patience while I pounded away at the keyboard. I appreciate your great sacrifice of my time while I got this thing done. Momma loves you guys immensely. I appreciate you, Debra, for reminding me that my destiny is to spread love, help, and motivation to those around me! You guys rock!

References

Education pays, 2022: Career Outlook: U.S. Bureau of Labor Statistics (bls.gov). https://www.bls.gov/careeroutlook/2023/data-on-display/education-pays.htm (Accessed 28 Jan. 2024.)

Glavin, Chris. *History of GED Testing | K12 Academics.* www.k12academics.com/academic-testing/ged-testing/history.

Indeed.com. (31 July 2021). "15 Top Qualities Employers Look for in Candidates". https://www.indeed.om/career-advice/finding-a-job/qualitis-employers-want. (Accessed February 2024)

Jeff Bergin and Lisa Ferrara. "How Student Attendance Can Improve Institutional Outcomes." *EDUCAUSE Review*, er.educause.edu/blogs/sponsored/2019/4/how-student-attendance-can-improve-institutional-outcomes. Accessed 26 Jan. 2024.

Response. "Non-Traditional Education - What Is It and How Can It Help? - Response," August 8, 2018. https://response.com/non-traditional-education/.

"The Benefits of Career and Technical Education Programs for High Schoolers." *U.S. News And World Report*, 22 Dec. 2022, www.usnews.com/education/k12/articles/the-benefits-of-career-and-technical-education-programs-for-high-schoolers.

"The Evolution of the GED: Eight Decades of Student Success - GED." *GED*, 22 Dec. 2022, ged.com/blog/the-evolution-of-the-ged-eight-decades-of-student-success.

ThinkImpact. (2021). *College Dropout Rates.* https://www.thinkimpact.com/college-dropout-rates/

"Understanding the U.S. Immigrant Experience: The 2023 KFF/LA Times Survey of Immigrants - Findings - 10217 | KFF." *KFF*, 16 Apr. 2024, www.kff.org/report-section/understanding-the-u-s-immigrant-experience-the-2023-kff-la-times-survey-of-immigrants-findings/#:~:text=About%20half%20of%20all%20immigrants%20have%20limited%20English,barriers%20in%20a%20variety%20of%20settings%20and%20interactions.

Printed and bound by CPI Group (UK) Ltd, Croydon, CR0 4YY

30/04/2025

01857728-0004